Mostly Muffins

Mostly Muffins

Barbara Albright and Leslie Weiner

Illustrations by Janet Nelson

ST. MARTIN'S PRESS · NEW YORK

MOSTLY MUFFINS.
Copyright © 1984 by Barbara Albright and Leslie Weiner.
All rights reserved.
Printed in the United States of America.
No part of this book may be used or reproduced
in any manner whatsoever without written permission
except in the case of brief quotations
embodied in critical articles or reviews.
For information, address St. Martin's Press,
175 Fifth Avenue, New York, N.Y. 10010.

Design by Janet Tingey

Library of Congress Cataloging in Publication Data

Albright, Barbara.
Mostly muffins.

1. Muffins.   I. Weiner, Leslie.   II. Title.
TX769.A485   1984   641.8′15   84-23735
ISBN 0-312-54916-4 (pbk.)

First Edition

10 9 8

To Lowell and Ted,
for their patience, support, encouragement, and tastebuds.
And to our parents,
for turning us loose in the kitchen at a young age.

Contents

Introduction

Mostly Muffins is a celebration of one of our favorite foods. This book gave us an excuse to create muffins of every flavor, and to taste-test them carefully (over 150 trials) with our friends. We would now like to share our favorites with you. In fact, we've already begun—en route to a "tasting," a bag of samples was inadvertently left in a New York City subway car!

The 61 muffin recipes in this book range from the all-time classics, such as Blueberry and Bran, to the decidedly decadent and extravagant, such as Marzipan Raspberry. There are recipes to satisfy every craving, from the sweet (try Chocolate Bourbon Muffins, page 42) to the hot and savory (indulge yourself with Pepperoni Pizza Muffins, page 74) to the nutritiously delicious (Cranberry Orange Muffins, page 12). To top them off, we have a special chapter devoted to spreads. We hope you'll be so inspired that you'll go on to create your own combinations with the guiding tips given in the final chapter. Most of the items in the book are quick and easy to prepare—two of the many merits of muffin cookery.

Muffins add a delightful homemade touch to any meal or snack. Their versatility is endless. In addition to being perfect for breakfast, muffins are wonderful with soup-and-salad meals. They are appealing to children and to the child in adults, because it's fun to have your own individual treat. And, the aroma of baking muffins is hard to resist.

Making Perfect Muffins

Muffin making is quick and easy. In forty minutes or less, you can be enjoying freshly baked muffins. And you probably have the necessary ingredients on hand for several recipes.

The term "muffin" has come to include any small, cakelike baked good that is made in a muffin tin. Most of our recipes are made according to the classic muffin method, but a few are made using other techniques.

Read each recipe through before preparing it. When measuring ingredients, make sure you use the appropriate measuring cups for dry and liquid ingredients. Use measuring spoons as opposed to flatware.

In general, to make muffins, the dry ingredients (such as flour, baking powder and/or baking soda, sugar, and salt) are stirred together in a bowl. Then, in another bowl, the liquid ingredients (such as milk, eggs, and melted butter and/or oil) are stirred together and poured into a well made in the center of the dry ingredients.

The most common leavening agent available today is double-acting baking powder, which enables leavening to occur at room temperature and during baking. It contains an acid component (calcium acid phosphate) and an alkali component (bicarbonate of soda). Adding liquid to baking powder causes a chemical reaction between the acid and alkali, forming carbon dioxide and water. Leavening occurs when heat causes carbon dioxide gas to be released into the batter.

When acid ingredients (such as buttermilk, yogurt, sour cream, citrus juices, cranberries, and molasses) are used in muffins, baking soda (bicarbonate of soda—an alkali) is usually necessary to balance the acid-alkali ratio. This ratio must be in proper proportion for optimal leavening to take place.

To create nicely textured, round-topped muffins, it's important that the batter not be overbeaten. Stir the mixture with a few strokes—a maximum of fifteen to twenty—just until no streaks of dry ingredients remain. It's almost a folding motion. There will probably be small lumps in the batter, which will disappear when the muffins are baked. If nuts or fruit are to be added, they should be mixed in with one or two quick strokes.

Depending upon the components, the consistency of the muffin batter can vary widely. Some batters are pourable, while others are quite stiff. Spoon batter evenly among muffin cups lightly greased with butter, vegetable shortening, or vegetable oil; paper liners can also be used, if desired. If muffins are to be jumbo sized, grease the edges surrounding the cups. Tap the pan on the counter a couple of times to settle batter. Fill unused cups with a few tablespoons of water to ensure even baking and to protect your pan.

Bake muffins in a fully preheated oven for the specified length of time, or until a cake tester inserted in the center of a muffin comes out clean. Our muffins are all baked in $3 \times 1\frac{1}{4}$-inch ($3\frac{1}{2}$- to 4-ounce) muffin cups. If you change the size cups to make jumbo or mini-muffins, the time will have to be varied accordingly.

Cool muffins in the tins 5 to 10 minutes, then remove to a wire rack. Serve warm, or cool muffins completely before storing. If necessary, loosen muffins from cups by running a knife around the edge of each cup. It's important to let the muffins stay in their cups for a short period so they don't break apart when removed, but they should not be left in for longer than 10 minutes, as the moisture they will accumulate around their bases may make them difficult to remove.

Perfect muffins should be tender and light and have a uniform texture and moist crumb. They should be straight-sided and rounded on top. And, of course, they should taste great! Overbeating muffin batter will cause the gluten in the flour to overdevelop, which will toughen the texture of the muffins and may fill them full of tunnels. Generally, muffins are baked in a 350°F to 425°F oven for approximately 15 to 30 minutes; if the oven heat is too low, the muffins may not peak properly, and too high an oven temperature can cause them to crack and peak unevenly.

It's difficult to resist freshly baked muffins, and they're best when eaten right away. Store any cooled leftovers in an airtight container at room temperature. Always refrigerate muffins that contain cheese or meat, and refrigerate all muffins during hot summer months. Most muffins also freeze well.

To reheat muffins, wrap them loosely in aluminum foil. Heat room-temperature or refrigerated muffins at 250°F for 5 to 10 minutes; heat frozen muffins at 350°F for 15 to 20 minutes.

Sweet Muffins

Fresh Fruit and Vegetable Muffins

· APPLE BRAN MUFFINS ·

1 cup plain yogurt
1/4 cup milk
3 tablespoons vegetable oil
1 egg, lightly beaten
1 teaspoon vanilla
1 cup bran morsels (such as Bran
    Buds)

1 1/4 cups whole-wheat flour
1/3 cup firmly packed dark-brown sugar
1 tablespoon baking powder
1 teaspoon ground cinnamon
1/4 teaspoon salt
1 1/2 cups coarsely chopped tart green
    apples

Preheat oven to 400°F. Grease ten 3 × 1 1/4-inch (3 1/2- to 4-ounce) muffin cups.

In a medium bowl, stir together yogurt, milk, oil, egg, and vanilla until blended. Stir in bran morsels and let stand 1 to 2 minutes, or until cereal is softened. Meanwhile, in another bowl, stir together flour, brown sugar, baking powder, cinnamon, and salt. Make a well in center of dry ingredients; add bran mixture and stir just to combine. Stir in apples.

Spoon batter into prepared muffin cups; bake 15 to 20 minutes, or until a cake tester inserted in center of one muffin comes out clean.

Remove muffin tin or tins to wire rack. Cool 5 minutes before removing

muffins from cups; finish cooling on rack. Serve warm or cool completely and store in an airtight container at room temperature.

Makes 10 muffins

· APPLE RAISIN MUFFINS ·

3/4 cup vegetable oil
1 cup sugar
2 eggs
1 teaspoon vanilla
2 cups all-purpose flour
3/4 teaspoon baking soda

3/4 teaspoon ground cinnamon
1/2 teaspoon salt
1 1/2 cups diced apples
1/2 cup raisins
1/2 cup chopped walnuts

Preheat oven to 400°F. Grease twelve 3 × 1 1/4-inch (3 1/2- to 4-ounce) muffin cups.

In a large bowl, beat oil and sugar with electric mixer for 2 minutes. Add eggs and vanilla; beat 1 minute. In another bowl, stir together flour, baking soda, cinnamon, and salt. Add dry ingredients to oil mixture; stir just to combine. Stir in apples, raisins, and walnuts.

Spoon batter into prepared muffin cups; bake 20 to 25 minutes or until a cake tester inserted in center of one muffin comes out clean.

Remove muffin tin or tins to wire rack. Cool 5 minutes before removing muffins from cups; finish cooling on rack. Serve warm or cool completely and store in an airtight container at room temperature.

These muffins freeze well.

Makes 12 muffins

· BLUEBERRY MUFFINS ·

2 cups all-purpose flour
1 cup plus 1 tablespoon sugar
2 teaspoons baking powder
1/2 teaspoon salt
1/2 cup milk
1/2 cup lightly salted butter or
  margarine, melted and cooled

1 egg, lightly beaten
1 teaspoon vanilla
2 cups fresh or thawed, drained frozen
  blueberries
1/2 cup walnut pieces (optional)

Preheat oven to 400°F. Grease twelve 3 × 1¼-inch (3½- to 4-ounce) muffin cups.

In a large bowl, stir together flour, 1 cup sugar, baking powder, and salt. In another bowl, stir together milk, butter, egg, and vanilla until blended. Make a well in center of dry ingredients; add milk mixture and stir just to combine. Mash ¼ cup blueberries and stir into batter with a few quick strokes. Stir in remaining blueberries and walnuts (if desired).

Spoon batter into prepared muffin cups and sprinkle with the remaining 1 tablespoon sugar. Bake 20 to 25 minutes, or until a cake tester inserted in center of one muffin comes out clean.

Remove muffin tin or tins to wire rack. Cool 5 minutes before removing muffins from cups; finish cooling on rack. Serve warm or cool completely and store in an airtight container at room temperature.

These muffins freeze well.

Makes 12 muffins

· CARROT CAKE MUFFINS ·

1¾ cups all-purpose flour
⅔ cup firmly packed light-brown sugar
1 teaspoon baking powder
½ teaspoon baking soda
½ teaspoon salt
1 teaspoon ground cinnamon
Dash ground mace

½ cup crushed pineapple in juice
½ cup vegetable oil
1 egg, lightly beaten
1½ teaspoons vanilla
2 cups shredded carrots
½ cup raisins

Preheat oven to 400°F. Grease twelve 3 × 1¼-inch (3½- to 4-ounce) muffin cups.

In a large bowl, stir together flour, brown sugar, baking powder, baking soda, salt, cinnamon, and mace. In another bowl, stir together pineapple, oil, egg, and vanilla until blended. Make a well in center of dry ingredients; add pineapple mixture and stir just to combine. Stir in carrots and raisins.

Spoon batter into prepared muffin cups; bake 15 to 20 minutes, or until a cake tester inserted in center of one muffin comes out clean.

Remove muffin tin or tins to wire rack. Cool 5 minutes before removing muffins from cups; finish cooling on rack. Serve warm or store completely cooled muffins in an airtight container at room temperature.

These muffins freeze well. (Delicious served with Cream Cheese Spread; see page 84.)

Makes 12 muffins

· CRANBERRY ORANGE MUFFINS ·

2 cups all-purpose flour
1/2 cup firmly packed light-brown sugar
1/2 cup vacuum-packed wheat germ
   with brown sugar and honey
2 teaspoons baking powder
1/2 teaspoon baking soda
1/2 teaspoon salt
1 cup chopped fresh or thawed,

   drained frozen cranberries
1/3 cup granulated sugar
3/4 cup orange juice
1/3 cup vegetable oil
1 egg, lightly beaten
1 1/2 teaspoons grated orange peel
1 teaspoon vanilla
1/2 cup chopped pecans

Preheat oven to 400°F. Grease twelve 3 × 1 1/4-inch (3 1/2- to 4-ounce) muffin cups.

In a large bowl, stir together flour, brown sugar, wheat germ, baking powder, baking soda, and salt. In a small bowl, stir together cranberries and granulated sugar; let stand 2 minutes. In a medium bowl, stir together orange juice, oil, egg, orange peel, and vanilla until blended. Make a well in center of dry ingredients; add cranberry mixture and orange juice mixture and stir just to combine. Stir in pecans.

Spoon batter into prepared muffin cups; bake 15 to 20 minutes, or until a cake tester inserted in center of one muffin comes out clean.

Remove muffin tin or tins to a wire rack. Cool 5 minutes before removing muffins from cups; finish cooling on rack. Serve warm or cool completely and store in an airtight container at room temperature.

These muffins freeze well.

Makes 12 muffins

· GINGER PEAR MUFFINS ·

2 cups all-purpose flour
1/2 cup firmly packed dark-brown sugar
1 teaspoon baking soda
1/2 teaspoon salt
2 teaspoons ground ginger
1 teaspoon ground cinnamon
1/8 teaspoon ground nutmeg
1/8 teaspoon ground cloves

1 container (8 ounces) plain yogurt
 (about 1 cup)
1/2 cup vegetable oil
3 tablespoons molasses
1 egg, lightly beaten
1 1/2 cups diced pears
1/2 cup raisins
1/3 cup chopped walnuts

Preheat oven to 400°F. Grease twelve 3 × 1¼-inch (3½- to 4-ounce) muffin cups.

In a large bowl, stir together flour, brown sugar, baking soda, salt, ginger, cinnamon, nutmeg, and cloves. In another bowl, stir together yogurt, oil, molasses, and egg until blended. Make a well in center of dry ingredients; add yogurt mixture and stir just to combine. Stir in pears, raisins, and walnuts.

Spoon batter into prepared muffin cups; bake 20 to 25 minutes, or until a cake tester inserted in center of one muffin comes out clean.

Remove muffin tin or tins to wire rack. Cool 5 minutes before removing muffins from cups; finish cooling on rack. Serve warm or cool completely and store in an airtight container at room temperature.

These muffins freeze well.

Makes 12 muffins

• JUMBO BANANA-NUT MUFFINS •

Because of their mega-size, these muffins are especially appealing for those who always want more. They're nutritiously delicious, so you needn't feel badly about eating the whole thing.

1 cup all-purpose flour
1 cup whole-wheat flour
1 teaspoon baking powder
1 teaspoon baking soda
1/4 teaspoon salt
1/2 cup lightly salted butter or
　margarine, softened

1/2 cup sugar
2 eggs
11/3 cups mashed ripe banana
1/4 cup milk
1 teaspoon vanilla
1 cup broken walnuts

Preheat oven to 375°F. Grease nine 3 × 11/4-inch (31/2- to 4-ounce) muffin cups and edges surrounding cups.

In a large bowl, stir together flours, baking powder, baking soda, and salt. In another bowl, cream butter and sugar until light and fluffy; beat in eggs. Stir in banana, milk, and vanilla. Add dry ingredients and stir just to combine; stir in walnuts.

Spoon batter into prepared muffin cups; bake 25 to 30 minutes or until a cake tester inserted in center of one muffin comes out clean.

Remove muffin tin or tins to wire racks. Cool 5 minutes before removing muffins from cups; finish cooling on rack. Serve warm or cool completely and store in an airtight container at room temperature.

These muffins freeze well.

Makes 9 muffins

· LEMON BLUEBERRY MUFFINS ·

2 cups all-purpose flour
²/₃ cup plus 1 tablespoon sugar
1 teaspoon baking powder
1 teaspoon baking soda
¹/₂ teaspoon salt
1 container (8 ounces) lemon yogurt
    (about 1 cup)

¹/₄ cup lightly salted butter or
    margarine, melted and cooled
1 egg, lightly beaten
1 to 2 teaspoons grated lemon peel
1 teaspoon vanilla
2 cups fresh or thawed, drained frozen
    blueberries

Preheat oven to 400°F. Grease twelve 3 × 1¹/₄-inch (3¹/₂- to 4-ounce) muffin cups.

In a large bowl, stir together flour, the ²/₃ cup sugar, baking powder, baking soda, and salt. In another bowl, stir together yogurt, butter, egg, lemon peel, and vanilla until blended. Make a well in center of dry ingredients; add yogurt mixture and stir just to combine. Stir in blueberries.

Spoon batter into prepared muffin cups and sprinkle with the remaining 1 tablespoon sugar. Bake 20 to 25 minutes, or until a cake tester inserted in center of one muffin comes out clean.

Remove muffin tin or tins to wire rack. Cool 5 minutes before removing muffins from cups; finish cooling on rack. Serve warm or cool completely and store in an airtight container at room temperature.

These muffins freeze well.

Makes 12 muffins

· PAPAYA CASHEW MUFFINS ·

3/4 cup vegetable oil
1 cup sugar
2 eggs
1 teaspoon vanilla
2 cups all-purpose flour
3/4 teaspoon baking soda

1/2 teaspoon salt
3/4 teaspoon ground cinnamon
1/8 teaspoon ground ginger
1 2/3 cups diced peeled papaya
1 1/4 cups lightly salted roasted cashews

Preheat oven to 400°F. Grease twelve 3 × 1 1/4-inch (3 1/2- to 4-ounce) muffin cups.

In a large bowl, beat oil and sugar with electric mixer for 2 minutes. Add eggs and vanilla; beat 1 minute. In another bowl, stir together flour, baking soda, salt, cinnamon, and ginger. Add dry ingredients to oil mixture; stir just to combine. Stir in papaya and cashews.

Spoon batter into prepared muffin cups; bake 20 to 25 minutes, or until a cake tester inserted in center of one muffin comes out clean.

Remove muffin tin or tins to wire rack. Cool 5 minutes before removing muffins from cups; finish cooling on rack. Serve warm or cool completely and store in an airtight container at room temperature.

These muffins freeze well.

Makes 12 muffins

· PEACH COCONUT MUFFINS ·

2 cups all-purpose flour
1/2 cup sugar
2 1/2 teaspoons baking powder
1/2 teaspoon salt
1/2 cup toasted flaked coconut (see note below)
2/3 cup toasted slivered almonds (see note below)

3/4 cup milk
1/3 cup vegetable oil
1 egg, lightly beaten
1 1/2 teaspoons vanilla
1 cup chopped, peeled fresh or thawed, drained frozen peaches

Preheat oven to 400°F. Grease twelve 3 × 1 1/4-inch (3 1/2- to 4-ounce) muffin cups.

In a large bowl, stir together flour, sugar, baking powder, and salt. Stir in coconut and almonds to coat. In another bowl, stir together milk, oil, egg, and vanilla until blended. Make a well in center of dry ingredients; add milk mixture and stir just to combine. Stir in peaches.

Spoon batter into prepared muffin cups; bake 20 to 25 minutes, or until a cake tester inserted in center of one muffin comes out clean.

Remove muffin tin or tins to wire rack. Cool 5 minutes before removing muffins from cups; finish cooling on rack. Serve warm or cool completely and store in an airtight container at room temperature.

These muffins freeze well.

Makes 12 muffins

Note: To toast coconut and almonds, place in single layer on baking sheet or jelly-roll pan. Bake at 350°F for 6 to 7 minutes, stirring once or twice until lightly browned.

• PUMPKIN PIE MUFFINS •

2 cups all-purpose flour
3/4 cup firmly packed dark-brown sugar
1 1/2 teaspoons baking powder
1/4 teaspoon baking soda
1/2 teaspoon salt
1 teaspoon ground cinnamon
1/2 teaspoon ground ginger
1/4 teaspoon ground cloves
1/8 teaspoon ground nutmeg
3/4 cup canned pumpkin

1/2 cup lightly salted butter or
*   margarine, melted and cooled*
1/4 cup buttermilk
2 eggs, lightly beaten
3 tablespoons molasses
1 teaspoon vanilla
3/4 cup coarsely chopped pecans or
*   walnuts*
3/4 cup chopped pitted dates

Preheat oven to 400°F. Grease twelve 3 × 1 1/4-inch (3 1/2- to 4-ounce) muffin cups.

In a large bowl, stir together flour, brown sugar, baking powder, baking soda, salt, cinnamon, ginger, cloves, and nutmeg. In another bowl, stir together pumpkin, butter, buttermilk, eggs, molasses, and vanilla until blended. Make a well in center of dry ingredients; add pumpkin mixture and stir just to combine. Stir in pecans and dates.

Spoon batter into prepared muffin cups; bake 20 to 25 minutes, or until a cake tester inserted in center of one muffin comes out clean.

Remove muffin tin or tins to wire rack. Cool 5 minutes before removing muffins from cups; finish cooling on rack. Serve them or cool completely and store in an airtight container at room temperature.

These muffins freeze very well.

Makes 12 muffins

· SWEET POTATO MUFFINS ·

1¾ cups all-purpose flour
⅓ cup sugar
2 teaspoons baking powder
½ teaspoon salt
1 teaspoon ground cinnamon
⅛ teaspoon ground nutmeg
¾ cup mashed baked sweet potato or
   yam, cooled
¾ cup pure maple syrup

2 eggs, lightly beaten
¼ cup lightly salted butter or
   margarine, melted and cooled
¼ cup vegetable oil
2 tablespoons water
1 teaspoon vanilla
½ cup chopped walnuts
½ cup raisins

Preheat oven to 400°F. Grease twelve 3 × 1¼-inch (3½- to 4-ounce) muffin cups.

In a large bowl, stir together flour, sugar, baking powder, salt, cinnamon, and nutmeg. In another bowl, stir together sweet potato, maple syrup, eggs, butter, oil, water, and vanilla until blended. Make a well in center of dry ingredients; add sweet potato mixture and stir just to combine. Stir in walnuts and raisins.

Spoon batter into prepared muffin cups; bake 20 to 25 minutes, or until a cake tester inserted in center of one muffin comes out clean.

Remove muffin tin or tins to wire rack. Cool 5 minutes before removing muffins from cups; finish cooling on rack. Serve warm or cool completely and store in an airtight container at room temperature.

These muffins freeze very well.

Makes 12 muffins

Dried Fruit / Nut Muffins

• APRICOT–BRAZIL NUT MUFFINS •

2 cups all-purpose flour
2/3 cup firmly packed light-brown sugar
2 teaspoons baking powder
1/2 teaspoon salt
1 cup chopped dried apricots
3/4 cup boiling water

1/2 cup vegetable oil
1/2 cup mashed ripe banana
1 egg, lightly beaten
1 teaspoon vanilla
1 cup coarsely chopped Brazil nuts

Preheat oven to 400°F. Grease twelve 3 × 1¼-inch (3½- to 4-ounce) muffin cups.

In a large bowl, stir together flour, brown sugar, baking powder, and salt. In another bowl, combine apricots with boiling water; let stand 5 minutes. Stir in oil, banana, egg, and vanilla until blended. Make a well in center of dry ingredients; add apricot mixture and stir just to combine. Stir in nuts.

Spoon batter into prepared muffin cups; bake 20 to 25 minutes, or until a cake tester inserted in center of one muffin comes out clean.

Remove muffin tin or tins to wire rack. Cool 5 minutes before removing muffins from cups; finish cooling on rack. Serve warm or cool completely and store in an airtight container at room temperature.

Makes 12 muffins

· APRICOT–PINE NUT MUFFINS ·

2 cups all-purpose flour
¹/₄ cup sugar
1 teaspoon baking soda
¹/₄ teaspoon salt
1 cup plain yogurt
¹/₄ cup milk
¹/₄ cup lightly salted butter or
   margarine, melted and cooled

1 egg, lightly beaten
2 tablespoons honey
1 teaspoon vanilla
³/₄ cup chopped dried apricots
¹/₂ cup (3 ounces) pine nuts, divided

Preheat oven to 400°F. Grease twelve 3 × 1¹/₄-inch (3¹/₂- to 4-ounce) muffin cups.

In a large bowl, stir together flour, sugar, baking soda, and salt. In another bowl, stir together yogurt, milk, butter, egg, honey, and vanilla until blended. Make a well in center of dry ingredients; add yogurt mixture and stir just to combine. Stir in apricots and all but 2 tablespoons of the pine nuts.

Spoon batter into prepared muffin cups and sprinkle with reserved pine nuts. Bake 15 to 20 minutes, or until a cake tester inserted in center of one muffin comes out clean.

Remove muffin tin or tins to wire rack. Cool 5 minutes before removing muffins from cups; finish cooling on rack. Serve warm or cool completely and store in an airtight container at room temperature.

These muffins freeze well.

Makes 12 muffins

· CHUNKY GRANOLA MUFFINS ·

2 cups granola
1 cup all-purpose flour
$^1/_3$ cup firmly packed light-brown sugar
2 teaspoons baking powder
$^1/_2$ teaspoon ground cinnamon
$^1/_2$ teaspoon salt
$^1/_2$ cup milk

$^1/_3$ cup lightly salted butter or
  margarine, melted and cooled
1 egg, lightly beaten
1 teaspoon vanilla
$^1/_2$ cup chopped pitted dates
$^1/_3$ cup slivered almonds
$^1/_4$ cup flaked coconut

Preheat oven to 400°F. Grease twelve 3 × 1$^1/_4$-inch (3$^1/_2$- to 4-ounce) muffin cups.

In a large bowl, stir together granola, flour, brown sugar, baking powder, cinnamon, and salt. In another bowl, stir together milk, butter, egg, and vanilla until blended. Make a well in center of dry ingredients; add milk mixture and stir just to combine. Stir in dates, almonds, and coconut.

Spoon batter into prepared muffin cups; bake 20 to 25 minutes, or until a cake tester inserted in center of one muffin comes out clean.

Remove muffin tin or tins to wire rack. Cool 5 minutes before removing muffins from cups; finish cooling on rack. Serve warm or cool completely and store in an airtight container at room temperature.

These muffins freeze well.

Makes 12 muffins

· DATE NUT MUFFINS ·

1 cup water
2 cups chopped pitted dates
1/3 cup firmly packed light-brown sugar
2 tablespoons honey
1/3 cup lightly salted butter or·
* margarine, melted and cooled*
1 egg, lightly beaten

1 tablespoon freshly squeezed lemon
  juice
1 teaspoon vanilla
2 cups all-purpose flour
1 1/2 teaspoons baking soda
1/2 teaspoon salt
1 cup chopped walnuts

Preheat oven to 400°F. Grease twelve 3 × 1¼-inch (3½- to 4-ounce) muffin cups.

In a small saucepan, bring water to a boil; remove from heat. Stir in dates, brown sugar, and honey; let stand 5 minutes. Stir butter into date mixture; let stand 15 minutes or until cooled, then stir in egg, lemon juice, and vanilla until blended.

In a large bowl, stir together flour, baking soda, and salt. Make a well in center of dry ingredients; add date mixture and stir just to combine. Stir in walnuts.

Spoon batter into prepared muffin cups; bake 15 to 20 minutes, or until a cake tester inserted in center comes out clean.

Remove muffin tin or tins to wire rack. Cool 5 minutes before removing muffins from cups; finish cooling on rack. Serve warm or cool completely and store in an airtight container at room temperature.

These muffins freeze well.

Makes 12 muffins

· HAWAIIAN MUFFINS ·

2 cups all-purpose flour
1/3 cup sugar
2 teaspoons baking powder
1/4 teaspoon salt
1 jar (3 1/2 ounces) salted, roasted
   macadamia nuts, chopped
   (about 1 cup)

2/3 cup flaked coconut
1/2 cup chopped dried pineapple
3/4 cup milk
1/2 cup lightly salted butter or
   margarine, melted and cooled
1 egg, lightly beaten
1 teaspoon vanilla

Preheat oven to 400°F. Grease twelve 3 × 1 1/4-inch (3 1/2- to 4-ounce) cups.

In a large bowl, stir together flour, sugar, baking powder, and salt; stir in nuts, coconut, and pineapple to coat. In another bowl, stir together milk, butter, egg, and vanilla until blended. Make a well in center of dry ingredients; add milk mixture and stir just to combine.

Spoon batter into prepared muffin cups; bake 15 to 20 minutes, or until a cake tester inserted in center of one muffin comes out clean.

Remove muffin tin or tins to wire rack. Cool 5 minutes before removing muffins from cups; finish cooling on rack. Serve warm or cool completely and store in an airtight container at room temperature.

These muffins freeze well. (Delicious served with Hawaiian Spread; see page 86.)

Makes 12 muffins

· HAZELNUT MUFFINS ·

2 cups all-purpose flour
1/2 cup sugar
1 1/2 teaspoons baking powder
1/2 teaspoon baking soda
1/4 teaspoon salt
1/2 cup buttermilk

1/2 cup hazelnut-flavored liqueur
1/3 cup lightly salted butter or
    margarine, melted and cooled
1 egg, lightly beaten
1 cup chopped hazelnuts (filberts)

Preheat oven to 400°F. Grease twelve 3 × 1 1/4-inch (3 1/2- to 4-ounce) muffin cups.

In a large bowl, stir together flour, sugar, baking powder, baking soda, and salt. In another bowl, stir together buttermilk, hazelnut-flavored liqueur, butter, and egg until blended. Make a well in center of dry ingredients; add buttermilk mixture and stir just to combine. Stir in hazelnuts.

Spoon batter into prepared muffin cups; bake 15 to 20 minutes, or until a cake tester inserted in center of one muffin comes out clean.

Remove muffin tin or tins to wire rack. Cool 5 minutes before removing muffins from cups; finish cooling on rack. Serve warm or cool completely and store in an airtight container at room temperature. (Delicious served with Hazelnut Cream-Cheese Spread; see page 87.)

Makes 12 muffins

· MAPLE WALNUT MUFFINS ·

2 cups all-purpose flour
2 tablespoons firmly packed
   dark-brown sugar
1½ teaspoons baking powder
½ teaspoon baking soda
¼ teaspoon salt
1 cup toasted chopped walnuts (see
   note below)

½ cup buttermilk
½ cup pure maple syrup
⅓ cup lightly salted butter or
   margarine, melted and cooled
1 egg, lightly beaten
½ teaspoon vanilla
½ teaspoon maple extract (optional)

Preheat oven to 400°F. Grease twelve 3 × 1¼-inch (3½- to 4-ounce) muffin cups.

In a large bowl, stir together flour, brown sugar, baking powder, baking soda, and salt; stir nuts into dry ingredients to coat. In another bowl, stir together buttermilk, syrup, butter, egg, vanilla, and maple extract (if desired; see Blueberry Muffins, page 10) until blended. Make a well in center of dry ingredients; add buttermilk mixture and stir just to combine.

Spoon batter into prepared muffin cups; bake 15 to 20 minutes or until a cake tester inserted in center of one muffin comes out clean.

Remove muffin tin or tins to wire rack. Cool 5 minutes before removing muffins from cups; finish cooling on rack. Serve warm or cool completely and store in an airtight container at room temperature.

These muffins freeze well.

Makes 12 muffins

Note: To toast walnuts, place in single layer on baking sheet or jelly-roll pan. Bake at 350°F for 6 to 7 minutes or until lightly browned, stirring once or twice.

· MINCEMEAT MUFFINS ·

2 cups all-purpose flour
1/3 cup sugar
2 teaspoons baking powder
1/2 teaspoon salt
1 1/4 cups prepared mincemeat

2 eggs, lightly beaten
1/3 cup water
1/3 cup vegetable oil
1 teaspoon vanilla
1 cup chopped walnuts

Preheat oven to 400°F. Grease twelve 3 × 1 1/4-inch (3 1/2- to 4-ounce) muffin cups.

In a large bowl, stir together flour, sugar, baking powder, and salt. In another bowl, stir together mincemeat, eggs, water, oil, and vanilla until blended. Make a well in center of dry ingredients; add mincemeat mixture and stir just to combine. Stir in walnuts.

Spoon batter into prepared muffin cups; bake 20 to 25 minutes, or until a cake tester inserted in center of one muffin comes out clean.

Remove muffin tin or tins to wire rack. Cool 5 minutes before removing muffins from cups; finish cooling on rack. Serve warm or cool completely and store in an airtight container in refrigerator. Let muffins reach room temperature or warm slightly before serving.

These muffins freeze very well.

Makes 12 muffins

Grain Muffins

· BOSTON BROWN BREAD MUFFINS ·

¹/₂ cup all-purpose flour
¹/₂ cup whole-wheat flour
¹/₂ cup rye flour
¹/₂ cup yellow cornmeal
¹/₄ cup sugar
1 teaspoon baking soda

¹/₂ teaspoon salt
³/₄ cup buttermilk
¹/₃ cup vegetable oil
¹/₃ cup molasses
1 egg, lightly beaten
1 cup raisins

Preheat oven to 400°F. Grease ten 3 × 1¹/₄-inch (3¹/₂- to 4-ounce) muffin cups.

In a large bowl, stir together flours, cornmeal, sugar, baking soda, and salt. In another bowl, stir together buttermilk, oil, molasses, and egg until blended. Make a well in center of dry ingredients; add buttermilk mixture and stir just to combine. Stir in raisins.

Spoon batter into prepared muffin cups; bake 15 to 20 minutes, or until a cake tester inserted in center of one muffin comes out clean.

Remove muffin tin or tins to wire rack. Cool 5 minutes before removing muffins from cups; finish cooling on rack. Serve warm or cool completely and store in an airtight container at room temperature.

Makes 10 muffins

· JUMBO BEST BRAN MUFFINS ·

1 cup buttermilk
2 eggs, lightly beaten
1/4 cup lightly salted butter or
    margarine, melted and cooled
1/4 cup vegetable oil
2 tablespoons honey
2 tablespoons molasses
1 1/2 cup bran morsels (such as Bran
    Buds)

1/2 cup unprocessed bran
1 cup whole-wheat flour
1/4 cup firmly packed dark-brown sugar
1 teaspoon baking powder
1 teaspoon baking soda
1/4 teaspoon salt
3/4 cup golden raisins

Preheat oven to 400°F. Grease eight 3 × 1¼-inch (3½- to 4-ounce) muffin
cups.

In a large bowl, stir together buttermilk, eggs, butter, oil, honey, and
molasses until blended; stir in bran morsels and unprocessed bran and let
stand 1 to 2 minutes, or until cereal is softened. Meanwhile, in another bowl,
stir together flour, brown sugar, baking powder, baking soda, and salt. Make
a well in center of dry ingredients; add bran mixture and stir just to combine.
Stir in raisins.

Spoon batter into prepared muffin cups; bake 20 to 25 minutes or until a
cake tester inserted in center of one muffin comes out clean.

Remove muffin tin or tins to wire rack. Cool 5 minutes before removing
muffins from cups; finish cooling on rack. Serve warm or cool completely and
store in an airtight container at room temperature.

These muffins freeze well.

Makes 8 muffins

· OAT BRAN MUFFINS ·

1 cup all-purpose flour
$^{1}/_{2}$ cup oat bran
$^{1}/_{2}$ cup uncooked old-fashioned rolled
   oats
$^{1}/_{3}$ cup firmly packed light-brown sugar
1 teaspoon baking powder
1 teaspoon baking soda
$^{1}/_{4}$ teaspoon salt

1 cup buttermilk
$^{1}/_{4}$ cup lightly salted butter or
   margarine, melted and cooled
1 egg, lightly beaten
2 tablespoons vegetable oil
1 teaspoon vanilla
$^{3}/_{4}$ cup chopped pitted dates
$^{3}/_{4}$ cup chopped walnuts

Preheat oven to 400°F. Grease nine 3 × 1¼-inch (3½- to 4-ounce) muffin cups.

In a large bowl, stir together flour, oat bran, rolled oats, brown sugar, baking powder, baking soda, and salt. In another bowl, stir together buttermilk, butter, egg, oil, and vanilla until blended. Make a well in center of dry ingredients; add buttermilk mixture and stir just to combine. Stir in dates and walnuts.

Spoon batter into prepared muffin cups; bake 15 to 20 minutes, or until a cake tester inserted in center of one muffin comes out clean.

Remove muffin tin or tins to wire rack. Cool 5 minutes before removing muffins from cups; finish cooling on rack. Serve warm or cool completely and store in an airtight container at room temperature.

Makes 9 muffins

· OATMEAL PRUNE MUFFINS ·

1 cup water
1½ cups chopped, pitted dried prunes
⅔ cup uncooked old-fashioned rolled
   oats
½ cup lightly salted butter or
   margarine, melted and cooled
1½ cups all-purpose flour
1 cup firmly packed light-brown sugar

1 teaspoon baking soda
½ teaspoon salt
1 teaspoon ground cinnamon
⅛ teaspoon ground nutmeg
2 eggs, lightly beaten
1 teaspoon vanilla
¼ teaspoon grated orange peel

Preheat oven to 400°F. Grease twelve 3 × 1¼-inch (3½- to 4-ounce) muffin cups.

In a small saucepan, bring water to a boil; remove from heat. Stir in prunes and oats; let stand 20 minutes. Stir in butter; let stand 10 minutes, or until cooled. In a large bowl, stir together flour, brown sugar, baking soda, salt, cinnamon, and nutmeg. Stir eggs, vanilla, and orange peel into prune mixture in saucepan. Make a well in center of dry ingredients; add prune mixture and stir just to combine.

Spoon batter into prepared muffin cups; bake 20 to 25 minutes, or until a cake tester inserted in center of one muffin comes out clean.

Remove muffin tin or tins to wire rack. Cool 5 minutes before removing muffins from cups; finish cooling on rack. Serve warm or cool completely and store in an airtight container at room temperature.

These muffins freeze well.

Makes 12 muffins

OATMEAL RAISIN
· SUNFLOWER-SEED MUFFINS ·

1 cup all-purpose flour
1 cup uncooked old-fashioned rolled
    oats
1/2 cup firmly packed light-brown sugar
2 1/2 teaspoons baking powder
1/2 teaspoon salt
1/2 cup milk

1 egg, lightly beaten
2 tablespoons lightly salted butter or
    margarine, melted and cooled
2 tablespoons vegetable oil
1 teaspoon vanilla
3/4 cup raisins
1/2 cup sunflower seeds

Preheat oven to 400°F. Grease nine 3 × 1¼-inch (3½- to 4-ounce) muffin
cups.

In a large bowl, stir together flour, oats, brown sugar, baking powder, and
salt. In another bowl, stir together milk, egg, butter, oil, and vanilla until
blended. Make a well in center of dry ingredients; add milk mixture and stir
just to combine. Stir in raisins and sunflower seeds.

Spoon batter into prepared muffin cups; bake 15 to 20 minutes, or until a
cake tester inserted in center of one muffin comes out clean.

Remove muffin tin or tins to wire rack. Cool 5 minutes before removing
muffins from cups; finish cooling on rack. Serve warm or cool completely and
store in an airtight container at room temperature.

These muffins freeze well.

Makes 9 muffins

· PUMPERNICKEL RAISIN MUFFINS ·

3/4 cup rye flour
1/2 cup all-purpose flour
1/3 cup firmly packed dark-brown sugar
1/4 cup yellow cornmeal
1 tablespoon unsweetened cocoa
  powder
1 teaspoon baking soda

1/4 teaspoon salt
1 cup buttermilk
1/4 cup lightly salted butter or
  margarine, melted and cooled
1 egg, lightly beaten
2 tablespoons molasses
1 cup raisins

Preheat oven to 400°F. Grease nine 3 × 1¼-inch (3½- to 4-ounce) muffin cups.

In a large bowl, stir together flours, brown sugar, cornmeal, cocoa, baking soda, and salt. In another bowl, stir together buttermilk, butter, egg, and molasses until blended. Make a well in center of dry ingredients; add buttermilk mixture and stir just to combine. Stir in raisins.

Spoon batter into prepared muffin cups; bake 15 to 20 minutes, or until a cake tester inserted in center of one muffin comes out clean.

Remove muffin tin or tins to a wire rack. Cool 5 minutes before removing muffins from cups; finish cooling on rack. Serve warm or cool completely and store in an airtight container at room temperature.

These muffins freeze well.

Makes 9 muffins

· SWEET CORN MUFFINS ·

1 1/4 cups all-purpose flour
3/4 cup yellow cornmeal
1/4 cup sugar
1 tablespoon baking powder
1/2 teaspoon salt
1 cup milk

1/2 cup vegetable oil
2 eggs, lightly beaten
2 tablespoons lightly salted butter or
    margarine, melted and cooled
2 tablespoons honey
1 teaspoon vanilla

Preheat oven to 400°F. Grease nine 3 × 1 1/4-inch (3 1/2- to 4-ounce) muffin cups.

In a large bowl, stir together flour, cornmeal, sugar, baking powder, and salt. In another bowl, stir together milk, oil, eggs, butter, honey, and vanilla until blended. Make a well in center of dry ingredients; add milk mixture and stir just to combine.

Spoon batter into prepared muffin cups; bake 15 to 20 minutes, or until a cake tester inserted in center comes out clean.

Remove muffin tin or tins to wire rack. Cool 5 minutes before removing muffins from cups; finish cooling on rack. Serve warm or cool completely and store in an airtight container at room temperature.

These muffins freeze well.

Makes 9 muffins

· THREE-GRAIN DATE MUFFINS ·

1 cup bran morsels (such as Bran
   Buds)
½ cup yellow cornmeal
½ cup uncooked old-fashioned rolled
   oats
¾ cup boiling water
1 cup buttermilk
¼ cup molasses
¼ cup lightly salted butter or
   margarine, melted and cooled

2 tablespoons honey
2 tablespoons vegetable oil
1 egg, lightly beaten
1½ teaspoons vanilla
1 cup whole-wheat flour
1½ teaspoons baking soda
¼ teaspoon salt
¾ cup chopped, pitted dates

Preheat oven to 375°F. Grease twelve 3 × 1¼-inch (3½- to 4-ounce) muffin
cups.

In a large bowl, stir together bran morsels, cornmeal, and oats; stir in
boiling water and let stand 5 minutes. Stir in buttermilk, molasses, butter,
honey, oil, egg, and vanilla until blended. In another large bowl, stir together
flour, baking soda, and salt. Make a well in center of dry ingredients; add
grain-buttermilk mixture and stir just to combine. Stir in dates.

Spoon batter into prepared muffin cups; bake 20 to 25 minutes, or until a
cake tester inserted in center of one muffin comes out clean.

Remove muffin tin or tins to wire rack. Cool 5 minutes before removing
muffins from cups; finish cooling on rack. Serve warm or cool completely and
store in an airtight container at room temperature.

These muffins freeze well.

Makes 12 muffins

· WHEAT-GERM BRAN MUFFINS ·

$^1/_3$ cup shredded bran cereal (such as
   All-Bran)
$^3/_4$ cup buttermilk
$^1/_4$ cup vegetable oil
1 egg, lightly beaten
1 tablespoon molasses
1 cup all-purpose flour

$^1/_3$ cup vacuum-packed wheat germ
   with brown sugar and honey
$^1/_3$ cup sugar
$^1/_4$ cup yellow cornmeal
1 teaspoon baking soda
$^1/_2$ teaspoon salt
$^1/_2$ cup golden raisins

Preheat oven to 400°F. Grease nine 3 × 1$^1/_4$-inch (3$^1/_2$- to 4-ounce) muffin cups.

In a small bowl, stir together cereal and buttermilk. Let stand 2 minutes, then stir in oil, egg, and molasses. In a large bowl, stir together flour, wheat germ, sugar, cornmeal, baking soda and salt. Make a well in center of dry ingredients; add cereal mixture and stir just to combine. Stir in raisins.

Spoon batter into prepared muffin cups; bake 15 to 20 minutes or until a cake tester inserted in center of one muffin comes out clean.

Remove muffin tin or tins to wire rack. Cool 5 minutes before removing muffins from cups; finish cooling on rack. Serve warm or cool completely and store in an airtight container at room temperature.

These muffins freeze well. (Delicious served with Orange Honey Butter; see page 90.)

Makes 9 muffins

Chocolate and Chocolate Chip Muffins

· BLACK BOTTOM MUFFINS ·

MUFFIN BATTER:
1 1/4 cups all-purpose flour
3/4 cup sugar
1/3 cup unsweetened cocoa powder
1/2 teaspoon baking soda
1/4 teaspoon salt
2/3 cup buttermilk
1/4 cup vegetable oil
1/4 cup lightly salted butter or
    margarine, melted and cooled
1 egg, lightly beaten
1 teaspoon vanilla

1/3 cup semisweet chocolate chips,
    chopped

TOPPING:
2 packages (3 ounces each) cream
    cheese, softened
1/4 cup sugar
1 egg, lightly beaten
1/8 teaspoon almond extract
1/4 cup toasted slivered almonds (see
    note below)

Preheat oven to 375°F. Grease twelve 3 × 1 1/4-inch (3 1/2- to 4-ounce) muffin cups.

In a large bowl, stir together flour, sugar, cocoa, baking soda, and salt. In another bowl, stir together buttermilk, oil, butter, egg, and vanilla until blended. Make a well in center of dry ingredients; add buttermilk mixture and stir just to combine. Stir in chips. Spoon batter into prepared muffin cups.

In a medium bowl, stir together cream cheese, sugar, egg, and almond extract until well blended; stir in almonds. Spoon mixture over chocolate batter in muffin cups. Bake 20 to 25 minutes, or until a cake tester inserted in center of one muffin comes out clean.

Remove muffin tin or tins to wire rack. Cool 5 minutes before removing muffins from cups; finish cooling on rack. Serve warm or cool completely and store in an airtight container in refrigerator. Let muffins reach room temperature before serving.

These muffins freeze well.

Makes 12 muffins

Note: To toast almonds, place in single layer on baking sheet or jelly-roll pan. Bake at 350°F for 6 to 7 minutes, or until lightly browned, stirring once or twice.

· BLACK FOREST MUFFINS ·

6 squares (1 ounce each) semisweet
   chocolate
1/4 cup lightly salted butter or
   margarine
1/2 cup buttermilk
1/2 cup sugar
1 egg, lightly beaten
2 tablespoons cherry brandy

1 1/2 teaspoons vanilla
1 package (12 ounces) frozen pitted
   dark sweet cherries, thawed,
   coarsely chopped, and drained
1 3/4 cups all-purpose flour
1 teaspoon baking soda
1/2 teaspoon salt

Preheat oven to 400°F. Grease twelve 3 × 1 1/4-inch (3 1/2- to 4-ounce) muffin cups.

In a small saucepan, melt chocolate with butter over low heat. Let stand 10 minutes, or until cooled.

In a small bowl, stir chocolate mixture with buttermilk, sugar, egg, brandy, and vanilla until blended; stir in cherries. In a large bowl, stir together flour, baking soda, and salt. Make a well in center of dry ingredients; add chocolate mixture and stir just to combine.

Spoon batter into prepared muffin cups; bake 20 to 25 minutes, or until a cake tester inserted in center of one muffin comes out clean.

Remove muffin tin or tins to wire rack. Cool 5 minutes before removing muffins from cups; finish cooling on rack. Serve warm or cool completely and store in an airtight container at room temperature.

These muffins freeze well.

Makes 12 muffins

· CAPPUCCINO CHIP MUFFINS ·

2 cups all-purpose flour
3/4 cup sugar
2 1/2 teaspoons baking powder
2 teaspoons instant espresso coffee
   powder
1/2 teaspoon salt
1/2 teaspoon ground cinnamon

1 cup milk (scalded and cooled, if
   desired)
1/2 cup lightly salted butter or
   margarine, melted and cooled
1 egg, lightly beaten
1 teaspoon vanilla
3/4 cup semisweet chocolate mini-chips

Preheat oven to 375°F. Grease twelve 3 × 1 1/4-inch (3 1/2- to 4-ounce) muffin cups.

In a large bowl, stir together flour, sugar, baking powder, espresso coffee powder, salt, and cinnamon. In another bowl, stir together milk, butter, egg, and vanilla until blended. Make a well in center of dry ingredients; add milk mixture and stir just to combine. Stir in chips.

Spoon batter into prepared muffin cups; bake 15 to 20 minutes or until a cake tester inserted in center of one muffin comes out clean.

Remove muffin tin or tins to wire rack. Cool 5 minutes before removing muffins from cups; finish cooling on rack. Serve warm or cool completely and store in an airtight container at room temperature.

These muffins freeze well. (Delicious served with Espresso Spread; see page 85.)

Makes 12 muffins

· CHOCOLATE BOURBON MUFFINS ·

³/4 cup all-purpose flour
¹/2 teaspoon baking soda
¹/4 teaspoon salt
¹/2 cup lightly salted butter or
  margarine, softened
¹/2 cup sugar
1 square (1 ounce) semisweet chocolate,
  melted

1 egg
1 tablespoon bourbon
1 teaspoon vanilla
¹/2 cup semisweet chocolate chips
¹/2 cup chopped pecans

Preheat oven to 400°F. Grease nine 3 × 1¹/4-inch (3¹/2- to 4-ounce) muffin cups.

In a medium bowl, stir together flour, baking soda, and salt. In a large bowl, cream butter and sugar together until light and fluffy; beat in chocolate, egg, bourbon, and vanilla. Add dry ingredients and beat just to combine; stir in chips and pecans.

Spoon batter into prepared muffin cups; bake 15 to 20 minutes, or until a cake tester inserted in center of one muffin comes out clean.

Remove muffin tin or tins to wire rack. Cool 5 minutes before removing muffins from cups; finish cooling on rack. Serve warm or cool completely and store in an airtight container at room temperature.

These muffins freeze well.

Makes 9 muffins

· CHOCOLATE CHIP MUFFINS ·

These muffins are chock-full of jumbo milk-chocolate chips and nuts—decidedly decadent and sure to give Amos a run for his money.

2 cups all-purpose flour
1/3 cup firmly packed light-brown sugar
1/3 cup granulated sugar
2 teaspoons baking powder
1/2 teaspoon salt
2/3 cup milk
1/2 cup lightly salted butter or
  margarine, melted and cooled

2 eggs, lightly beaten
1 teaspoon vanilla
1 package (11.5 ounces) jumbo or
  regular-sized milk-chocolate chips
  (about 2 cups)
1/2 cup chopped walnuts or pecans

Preheat oven to 400°F. Grease twelve 3 × 1¼-inch (3½- to 4-ounce) muffin cups.

In a large bowl, stir together flour, sugars, baking powder, and salt. In another bowl, stir together milk, eggs, butter, and vanilla until blended. Make a well in center of dry ingredients; add milk mixture and stir just to combine. Stir in chocolate chips and nuts.

Spoon batter into prepared muffin cups; bake 15 to 20 minutes, or until a cake tester inserted in center of one muffin comes out clean.

Remove muffin tin or tins to wire rack. Cool 5 minutes before removing muffins from cups; finish cooling on rack. Serve warm or cool completely and store in an airtight container at room temperature.

These muffins freeze well.

Makes 12 muffins

· CHOCOLATE CHOCOLATE CHIP MUFFINS ·

6 squares (1 ounce each) semisweet
   chocolate
1/3 cup lightly salted butter or
   margarine
3/4 cup buttermilk
1/2 cup sugar

1 egg, lightly beaten
1 1/2 teaspoons vanilla
1 2/3 cups all-purpose flour
1 teaspoon baking soda
1/2 teaspoon salt
1 cup milk-chocolate chips

Preheat oven to 400°F. Grease twelve 3 × 1 1/4-inch (3 1/2- to 4-ounce) muffin cups.

In a small saucepan, melt chocolate with butter over low heat. Let stand 10 minutes, or until cooled.

In a small bowl, stir chocolate mixture with buttermilk, sugar, egg, and vanilla until blended. In a large bowl, stir together flour, baking soda, and salt. Make a well in center of dry ingredients; add chocolate mixture and stir just to combine. Stir in chips.

Spoon batter into prepared muffin cups; bake 20 to 25 minutes, or until a cake tester inserted in center of one muffin comes out clean.

Remove muffin tin or tins to wire rack. Cool 5 minutes before removing muffins from cups; finish cooling on rack. Serve warm or cool completely and store in an airtight container at room temperature.

These muffins freeze well.

Makes 12 muffins

· FOUR-CHIP DOUBLE-NUT MUFFINS ·

2 cups all-purpose flour
1/2 cup firmly packed light-brown sugar
2 teaspoons baking powder
1/2 teaspoon salt
2/3 cup milk
1/2 cup lightly salted butter or
    margarine, melted and cooled
2 eggs, lightly beaten

1 teaspoon vanilla
1/2 cup semisweet chocolate chips
1/2 cup milk-chocolate chips
1/2 cup butterscotch chips
1/2 cup peanut butter chips
1/3 cup chopped walnuts
1/3 cup chopped pecans

Preheat oven to 400°F. Grease twelve 3 × 1¼-inch (3½- to 4-ounce) muffin cups.

In a large bowl, stir together flour, brown sugar, baking powder, and salt. In another bowl, stir together milk, butter, eggs, and vanilla until blended. Make a well in center of dry ingredients; add milk mixture and stir just to combine. Stir in chips and nuts.

Spoon batter into prepared muffin cups; bake 15 to 20 minutes, or until a cake tester inserted in center of one muffin comes out clean.

Remove muffin tin or tins to wire rack. Cool 5 minutes before removing muffins from cups; finish cooling on rack. Serve warm or cool completely and store in an airtight container at room temperature.

These muffins freeze well.

Makes 12 muffins

· ORANGE CHOCOLATE CHIP MUFFINS ·

2 cups all-purpose flour
1/2 cup firmly packed light-brown sugar
1/2 cup granulated sugar
1 1/2 teaspoons baking powder
1/2 teaspoon baking soda
1/2 teaspoon salt
1/3 cup vegetable oil

1/4 cup orange juice
1/4 cup orange-flavored liqueur (such as
    Grand Marnier)
1 egg, lightly beaten
1 teaspoon grated orange peel
1 teaspoon vanilla
1 cup semisweet chocolate chips

Preheat oven to 400°F. Grease ten 3 × 1 1/4-inch (3 1/2- to 4-ounce) muffin cups.

In a large bowl, stir together flour, sugars, baking powder, baking soda, and salt. In another bowl, stir together oil, juice, liqueur, egg, orange peel, and vanilla. Make a well in center of dry ingredients; add oil mixture and stir just to combine. Stir in chips.

Spoon batter into prepared muffin cups; bake 15 to 20 minutes, or until a cake tester inserted in center of one muffin comes out clean.

Remove muffin tin or tins to wire rack. Cool 5 minutes before removing muffins from cups; finish cooling on rack. Serve warm or cool completely and store in an airtight container at room temperature.

These muffins freeze well.

Makes 10 muffins

Sweet Specialty Muffins

· CRUMBCAKE MUFFINS ·

TOPPING:

1 cup all-purpose flour
1/3 cup lightly salted butter or margarine, softened
1/3 cup firmly packed light-brown sugar
1/4 teaspoon ground cinnamon

MUFFIN BATTER:

1 3/4 cups all-purpose flour
3/4 cup granulated sugar
1 3/4 teaspoons baking powder
1/2 teaspoon salt
1 cup milk
1/2 cup lightly salted butter or margarine, melted and cooled
1 egg, plus 1 egg yolk, lightly beaten
1 teaspoon vanilla
1/4 teaspoon almond extract

3 tablespoons confectioners sugar

Preheat oven to 400°F. Grease twelve 3 × 1 1/4-inch (3 1/2- to 4-ounce) muffin cups.

In a small bowl, stir together topping ingredients (flour, softened butter, brown sugar, and cinnamon) until mixture resembles coarse crumbs; set topping aside.

In a large bowl, stir together flour, granulated sugar, baking powder, and salt. In another bowl, stir together milk, melted butter, egg, egg yolk, vanilla, and almond extract until blended. Make a well in center of dry ingredients; add milk mixture and stir just to combine.

Spoon batter into prepared muffin cups; sprinkle an equal amount of crumb topping over each muffin. Bake 20 to 25 minutes, or until cake tester inserted in center of one muffin comes out clean.

Remove muffin tin or tins to wire rack. Cool 5 minutes before removing muffins from cups; finish cooling on rack. Sift confectioners sugar over muffins. Serve warm or cool completely and store in an airtight container at room temperature.

These muffins freeze well (if frozen, thaw before adding confectioners sugar). Delicious served with any of our sweet spreads.

Makes 12 muffins

· FIG MUFFINS ·

A classic done in muffin form.

FIG FILLING:
1/2 pound dried figs, trimmed and chopped
1/2 cup freshly squeezed orange juice
3 tablespoons honey
1 1/2 teaspoons freshly squeezed lemon juice

MUFFIN BATTER:
1 1/4 cups all-purpose flour
3/4 cup whole-wheat flour
1 teaspoon baking powder
1/2 teaspoon baking soda
1/2 teaspoon salt
1/2 cup lightly salted butter or margarine, melted and cooled
1/2 cup firmly packed dark-brown sugar
1/4 cup honey
1 egg, lightly beaten
3/4 cup freshly squeezed orange juice

In a small saucepan, combine filling ingredients (figs, 1/2 cup orange juice, 3 tablespoons honey, and lemon juice); bring to a boil. Reduce heat, cover, and simmer 20 minutes, stirring occasionally. Remove cover and return to a boil; boil 1 to 3 minutes, or until thickened. Remove from heat; cool slightly.

Scrape fig mixture into container of food processor fitted with steel blade. Process 30 seconds or until puréed, stopping to scrape down sides of container with rubber scraper, if necessary. Remove to a small bowl; you should have about 1 cup filling. Cover and chill at least 1 hour before using.

Preheat oven to 400°F. Grease twelve 3 × 1¼-inch (3½- to 4-ounce) muffin cups.

In a large bowl, stir together flours, baking powder, baking soda, and salt. In another bowl, stir together butter, brown sugar, and ¼ cup honey. Stir in egg and ¾ cup orange juice. Make a well in center of dry ingredients; add butter mixture and stir just to combine.

Spoon half of batter into prepared muffin cups.

Divide fig filling among muffin cups, about 1½ tablespoons per cup; do not let filling touch sides of cups. Spoon remaining batter into cups over filling; bake 15 to 20 minutes, or until lightly browned.

Remove muffin tin or tins to wire rack. Cool 5 minutes before removing muffins from cups; finish cooling on rack. Serve warm or cool completely and store in an airtight container at room temperature.

These muffins freeze well.

Makes 12 muffins

FUDGE-FILLED
PEANUT BUTTER MUFFINS

$^1/_3$ cup semisweet chocolate chips
1 tablespoon unsalted (sweet) butter or
    margarine
$1^2/_3$ cups all-purpose flour
$^1/_2$ cup firmly packed light-brown sugar
1 tablespoon baking powder
$^1/_4$ teaspoon salt

$^3/_4$ cup milk
$^1/_2$ cup peanut butter
$^1/_3$ cup vegetable oil
1 egg, lightly beaten
$1^1/_2$ teaspoons vanilla
$^1/_2$ cup chopped salted peanuts without
    skins (optional)

Preheat oven to 400°F. Grease nine 3 × 1¼-inch (3½- to 4-ounce) muffin
cups.

In a small saucepan, heat chocolate chips and butter until melted, stirring
constantly; remove from heat and reserve.

In a large bowl, stir together flour, brown sugar, baking powder, and salt.
In another bowl, stir together milk, peanut butter, oil, egg, and vanilla until
blended. Make a well in center of dry ingredients; add milk mixture and stir
just to combine.

Spoon half of batter into prepared muffin cups. Divide chocolate mixture
among muffin cups, scant teaspoon per cup; do not let filling touch sides of
cup. Spoon remaining batter into cups over filling. Sprinkle tops of muffins
with chopped peanuts, if desired. Bake 20 to 25 minutes, or until lightly
browned.

Remove muffin tin or tins to wire rack. Cool 5 minutes before removing

muffins from cups; finish cooling on rack. Serve warm or cool completely and store in an airtight container at room temperature.

Makes 9 muffins

Note: If desired, one ripe banana, cut into $1/2$-inch thick slices and dipped in orange juice, can be used instead of the chocolate filling.

· GINGERBREAD MUFFINS ·

1¼ cups all-purpose flour
½ cup whole-wheat flour
½ cup firmly packed light-brown sugar
2 teaspoons ground ginger
1 teaspoon baking soda
¼ teaspoon salt
1 teaspoon ground cinnamon

⅛ teaspoon ground cloves
⅛ teaspoon ground nutmeg
¾ cup buttermilk
½ cup vegetable oil
2 eggs, lightly beaten
¼ cup molasses
1 cup currants

Preheat oven to 400°F. Grease twelve 3 × 1¼-inch (3½- to 4-ounce) muffin cups.

In a large bowl, stir together flours, brown sugar, ginger, baking soda, salt, cinnamon, cloves, and nutmeg. In another bowl, stir together buttermilk, oil, eggs, and molasses until blended. Make a well in center of dry ingredients; add buttermilk mixture and stir just to combine. Stir in currants.

Spoon batter into prepared muffin cups; bake 15 to 20 minutes, or until a cake tester inserted in center of one muffin comes out clean.

Remove muffin tin or tins to wire rack. Cool 5 minutes before removing muffins from cups; finish cooling on rack. Serve warm or cool completely and store in an airtight container at room temperature.

These muffins freeze well. (Delicious served with Lemon Glaze; see page 88.)

Makes 12 muffins

· GRAHAM CRACKER MUFFINS ·

1 cup all-purpose flour
1/2 cup graham cracker crumbs
1/2 cup vacuum-packed wheat germ
   with brown sugar and honey
1/4 cup whole-wheat flour
1/4 cup sugar
1 1/4 teaspoons baking soda

1/2 teaspoon salt
1 cup buttermilk
1/3 cup molasses
1/3 cup vegetable oil
1 egg, lightly beaten
1/2 cup raisins

Preheat oven to 400°F. Grease twelve 3 × 1 1/4-inch (3 1/2- to 4-ounce) muffin cups.

In a large bowl, stir together flour, graham cracker crumbs, wheat germ, whole-wheat flour, sugar, baking soda, and salt. In another bowl, stir together buttermilk, molasses, oil, and egg. Make a well in center of dry ingredients; add buttermilk mixture and stir just to combine. Stir in raisins.

Spoon batter into prepared muffin cups; bake 15 to 20 minutes, or until a cake tester inserted in center of one muffin comes out clean.

Remove muffin tin or tins to wire rack. Cool 5 minutes before removing muffins from tins; finish cooling on rack. Serve warm or cool completely and store in an airtight container at room temperature.

These muffins freeze well.

Makes 12 muffins

· HOT CROSS MUFFINS ·

An easy-to-make substitute for hot cross buns.

2 cups all-purpose flour
3/4 cup sugar
2 teaspoons baking powder
1/2 teaspoon salt
1/4 teaspoon ground cinnamon
1/8 teaspoon ground allspice
1 cup milk
1/2 cup lightly salted butter or
  margarine, melted and cooled
1 egg, lightly beaten

1 teaspoon vanilla
1/2 teaspoon grated orange peel
1/4 teaspoon grated lemon peel
1 cup currants

GLAZE:
1/3 cup confectioners sugar
1 1/2 teaspoons freshly squeezed lemon
  juice or orange juice, or water

Preheat oven to 375°F. Grease twelve 3 × 1 1/4-inch (3 1/2- to 4-ounce) muffin cups.

In a large bowl, stir together flour, sugar, baking powder, salt, cinnamon, and allspice. In a small bowl, stir together milk, butter, egg, vanilla, orange peel, and lemon peel. Make a well in center of dry ingredients; add milk mixture and stir just to combine. Stir in currants.

Spoon batter into prepared muffin cups; bake 15 to 20 minutes, or until a cake tester inserted in center of one muffin comes out clean.

Remove muffin tin or tins to wire rack. Cool 5 minutes before removing muffins from cups; finish cooling on rack. For glaze, combine confectioners sugar and lemon juice. Drizzle over each muffin to form a cross. Serve warm or store completely cooled muffins in an airtight container at room temperature.

These muffins freeze well.

Makes 12 muffins

· LINZERTORTE MUFFINS ·

2 cups all-purpose flour
2 teaspoons baking powder
1/2 teaspoon salt
1 teaspoon ground cinnamon
1/8 teaspoon ground cloves
1/2 cup firmly packed dark-brown sugar
1/4 cup granulated sugar
1/2 cup lightly salted butter or
  margarine, softened

1 egg, lightly beaten
1 teaspoon grated lemon peel
1/2 teaspoon vanilla
1 cup milk
3/4 cup ground blanched hazelnuts
  (filberts)
1/4 cup seedless raspberry jam

Preheat oven to 400°F. Grease twelve 3 × 1¼-inch (3½- to 4-ounce) muffin cups.

In a large bowl, stir together flour, baking powder, salt, cinnamon, and cloves. In another bowl, cream sugars with butter until light and fluffy; beat in egg, lemon peel, and vanilla. Stir in milk. Make a well in center of dry ingredients; add butter mixture and stir just to combine. Stir in hazelnuts.

Spoon half of batter into prepared muffin cups. Place 1 teaspoon jam in center of each portion of batter; do not let jam touch sides of cups. Spoon remaining batter into cups over jam; bake 15 to 20 minutes, or until lightly browned.

Remove muffin tin or tins to wire rack. Cool 5 minutes before removing muffins from cups; finish cooling on rack. Serve warm or cool completely and store in an airtight container at room temperature.

These muffins freeze well.

Makes 12 muffins

• MARZIPAN RASPBERRY MUFFINS •

1 package (7 ounces) almond paste
2 tablespoons seedless raspberry jam
2 cups all-purpose flour
²/₃ cup sugar
2 teaspoons baking powder
¹/₂ teaspoon salt
1 cup milk

¹/₂ cup lightly salted butter or
   margarine, melted and cooled
1 egg, lightly beaten
1 teaspoon vanilla
¹/₄ teaspoon almond extract
³/₄ cup flaked coconut
24 whole blanched almonds

Preheat oven to 400°F. Grease twelve 3 × 1¹/₄-inch (3¹/₂- to 4-ounce) muffin cups.

Slice almond paste into 24 equal pieces; form each piece into 1¹/₂-inch diameter circle. Top center of twelve circles with ¹/₂ teaspoon jam; top with remaining circles and press edges to seal. Set pockets aside.

In a large bowl, stir together flour, sugar, baking powder, and salt. In another bowl, stir together milk, butter, egg, vanilla, and almond extract until blended. Make a well in center of dry ingredients; add milk mixture and stir just to combine. Stir in coconut.

Spoon half of batter into prepared muffin cups. Place a jam-filled almond paste "pocket" horizontally on top of each portion of filling; do not let almond paste touch sides of cups. Spoon remaining batter into cups over almond paste; top each muffin with almonds. Bake 15 to 20 minutes, or until lightly browned.

Remove muffin tin or tins to wire rack. Cool 5 minutes before removing

muffins from cups; finish cooling on rack. Serve warm or cool completely and store in an airtight container at room temperature.

These muffins freeze well.

Makes 12 muffins

Note: Muffins can also be prepared by cutting almond paste into 12 equal pieces and rolling each into a ball. Use this as the filling, without the jam; proceed as above. Serve muffins with jam.

• POPPY SEED MUFFINS •

2 cups all-purpose flour
1/4 cup poppy seed
1/2 teaspoon salt
1/4 teaspoon baking soda
1 cup sugar

1/2 cup lightly salted butter or
   margarine, softened
2 eggs
3/4 cup sour cream
1 teaspoon vanilla

Preheat oven to 375°F. Grease twelve 3 × 1 1/4-inch (3 1/2- to 4-ounce) muffin cups.

In a small bowl, stir together flour, poppy seed, salt, and baking soda. In a large bowl, beat sugar and butter with electric mixer for 2 minutes. Beat in eggs, one at a time, until blended; beat in sour cream and vanilla. Gradually beat in flour mixture until well combined.

Spoon batter into prepared muffin cups; bake 15 to 20 minutes, or until a cake tester inserted in center of one muffin comes out clean.

Remove muffin tin or tins to wire rack. Cool 5 minutes before removing muffins from cups; finish cooling on rack. Serve warm or cool completely and store in an airtight container at room temperature.

These muffins freeze well.

Makes 12 muffins

· POUNDCAKE MUFFINS ·

1 3/4 cups all-purpose flour
1/2 teaspoon salt
1/4 teaspoon baking soda
1 cup sugar
1/2 cup lightly salted butter or
    margarine, softened

1/2 cup sour cream
1 teaspoon vanilla
1/2 teaspoon lemon extract (optional)
2 eggs

Preheat oven to 400°F. Grease nine 3 × 1 1/4-inch (3 1/2- to 4-ounce) muffin cups.

In a small bowl, stir together flour, salt, and baking soda. In a large bowl, beat sugar and butter with electric mixer until well combined. Beat in sour cream, vanilla, and lemon extract (if desired) until well blended. Beat in eggs, one at a time, until well blended. Beat in dry ingredients until combined.

Spoon batter into prepared muffin cups; bake 20 to 25 minutes, or until a cake tester inserted in center of one muffin comes out clean.

Remove muffin tin or tins to wire rack. Cool 5 minutes before removing muffins from cups; finish cooling on rack. Serve warm or store completely cooled muffins in an airtight container at room temperature.

These muffins freeze well. (Delicious served with any of our sweet spreads, or split and serve with sliced strawberries and whipped cream.)

Makes 9 muffins

· SESAME MUFFINS ·

2 cups all-purpose flour
2 teaspoons baking powder
1/2 teaspoon salt
1/3 cup tahini (sesame seed paste,
    available in health food stores,
    Middle Eastern markets, and
    large supermarkets)
1/4 cup lightly salted butter or
    margarine, melted and cooled

1/2 teaspoon Oriental-style (dark)
    sesame oil
3/4 cup firmly packed light-brown sugar
1/2 cup milk
2 eggs, lightly beaten
1 teaspoon vanilla
2/3 cup raisins (optional)
4 tablespoons toasted sesame seeds,
    divided (see note below)

Preheat oven to 400°F. Grease twelve 3 × 1¼-inch (3½- to 4-ounce) muffin cups.

In a large bowl, stir together flour, baking powder, and salt. In another bowl, stir together tahini, butter, and oil; stir in sugar, milk, eggs, and vanilla until blended. Make a well in center of dry ingredients; add tahini mixture and stir just to combine. Stir in raisins and 3 tablespoons of the sesame seeds.

Spoon batter into prepared muffin cups; sprinkle with remaining 1 tablespoon sesame seeds. Bake 15 to 20 minutes, or until a cake tester inserted in center of one muffin comes out clean.

Remove muffin tin or tins to wire rack. Cool 5 minutes before removing muffins from tins; finish cooling on rack. Serve warm or cool completely and store in an airtight container at room temperature.

Makes 12 muffins

Note: To toast sesame seeds, place in small skillet over medium heat. Cook, stirring, for 3 minutes, or until seeds are lightly browned.

Savory Muffins

· BACON CHEDDAR MUFFINS ·

Great for breakfast and perfect with a bowl of soup and a tossed green salad.

1³/₄ cups all-purpose flour
¹/₃ cup yellow cornmeal
2 tablespoons sugar
2 teaspoons baking powder
¹/₈ teaspoon salt
Dash ground red pepper (see note below)
8 slices bacon, cooked, drained, cooled, and chopped (about ¹/₂ cup)
¹/₂ cup (about 2 ounces) shredded extra-sharp Cheddar cheese
1 cup milk
1 egg, lightly beaten
3 tablespoons lightly salted butter or margarine, melted and cooled
¹/₂ teaspoon Dijon-style mustard

Preheat oven to 400°F. Grease ten 3 × 1¹/₄-inch (3¹/₂- to 4-ounce) muffin cups.

In a large bowl, stir together flour, cornmeal, sugar, baking powder, salt, and red pepper; stir in bacon and cheese to coat. In another bowl, stir together milk, egg, butter, and mustard until blended. Make a well in center of dry ingredients; add milk mixture and stir just to combine. Spoon batter into prepared muffin cups; bake 20 to 25 minutes, or until a cake tester inserted in center of one muffin comes out clean.

Remove muffin tin or tins to wire rack. Cool 5 minutes before removing muffins from cups. Finish cooling on rack. Serve warm or cool completely and store in an airtight container in refrigerator. Let muffins reach room temperature or warm slightly before serving.

Makes 10 muffins
Note: For a hotter flavor, use ¹/₈ teaspoon ground red pepper.

· BEER CHEESE MUFFINS ·

1 cup beer
1 cup golden raisins
1 1/2 cups all-purpose flour
1 cup whole-wheat flour
1 1/4 cups (about 5 ounces) shredded
  Swiss cheese
2/3 cup sugar

1 1/2 teaspoons baking soda
1/4 to 1/2 teaspoon nutmeg
1/4 teaspoon salt
2 eggs, lightly beaten
1/4 cup lightly salted butter or
  margarine, melted and cooled
1 cup broken walnuts

Preheat oven to 400°F. Grease twelve 3 × 1 1/4-inch (3 1/2- to 4-ounce) muffin cups.

In a small saucepan, heat beer to boiling; remove from heat. Add raisins and let cool.

In a large bowl, stir together flours, cheese, sugar, baking soda, nutmeg, and salt. In another bowl, stir together beer-raisin mixture, eggs, and butter until blended. Make a well in center of dry ingredients; add beer mixture and stir just to combine. Stir in walnuts.

Spoon batter into prepared muffin cups; bake 15 to 20 minutes, or until a cake tester inserted in center of one muffin comes out clean.

Remove muffin tin or tins to wire rack. Cool 5 minutes before removing muffins from cups; finish cooling on rack. Serve warm or cool completely and store in an airtight container in refrigerator. Let muffins reach room temperature or warm slightly before serving.

These muffins freeze well.

Makes 12 muffins

· BOURSIN CHEESE MUFFINS ·

Try these with hors d'oeuvres.

2 cups all-purpose flour
2 teaspoons baking powder
1/8 teaspoon salt
Dash ground black pepper
1 package (5 ounces) Boursin cheese,
   softened
2 tablespoons lightly salted butter or
   margarine, softened

1 cup milk
1 egg, lightly beaten
1/2 cup chopped walnuts
3 tablespoons finely chopped scallions
1 clove garlic, minced

Preheat oven to 400°F. Grease twelve 3 × 1 1/4-inch (3 1/2- to 4-ounce) muffin cups.

In a large bowl, stir together flour, baking powder, salt, and pepper. In another bowl, cream Boursin cheese and butter together; beat in milk and egg. Add dry ingredients and beat just to combine; stir in walnuts, scallions, and garlic.

Spoon batter into prepared muffin cups; bake 20 to 25 minutes, or until a cake tester inserted in center of one muffin comes out clean.

Remove muffin tin or tins to wire rack. Cool 5 minutes before removing muffins from cups; finish cooling on rack. Serve warm or cool completely and store in an airtight container in refrigerator. Let muffins reach room temperature or warm slightly before serving.

Makes 12 muffins

· DOUBLE CORN MUFFINS ·

An excellent accompaniment for Tex-Mex fare.

1 cup all-purpose flour
1 cup yellow cornmeal
2 tablespoons sugar
2½ teaspoons baking powder
½ teaspoon salt
¼ teaspoon dry mustard
⅛ teaspoon ground black pepper
1 cup milk

½ cup corn or vegetable oil
2 eggs, lightly beaten
1½ to 3 teaspoons finely chopped onion
1 can (8¾-ounce) whole-kernel corn, drained, or 1 cup fresh corn, or thawed, drained frozen whole-kernel corn

Preheat oven to 400°F. Grease twelve 3 × 1¼-inch (3½- to 4-ounce) muffin cups.

In a large bowl, stir together flour, cornmeal, sugar, baking powder, salt, mustard, and pepper. In another bowl, stir together milk, oil, eggs and onion until blended. Make a well in center of dry ingredients; add milk mixture and stir just to combine. Stir in corn.

Spoon batter into prepared muffin cups; bake 15 to 20 minutes or until a cake tester inserted in center of one muffin comes out clean.

Remove muffin tin or tins to wire rack. Cool 5 minutes before removing muffins from cups; finish cooling on rack. Serve warm or cool completely and store in an airtight container at room temperature.

Makes 12 muffins

· ENGLISH MUFFINS ·

We couldn't do a cookbook on muffins without including a recipe for these favorites. While still called a muffin, English muffins are entirely different and especially delicious with the spreads.

4½ to 5 cups all-purpose flour
1 tablespoon sugar
1 package (¼ ounce) active dry yeast
1 teaspoon salt
1½ cups milk

3 tablespoons lightly salted butter or
   margarine
1 egg
3 tablespoons white or yellow cornmeal
Vegetable oil

In a large bowl, stir together 1½ cups of the flour, the sugar, yeast, and salt. In a medium saucepan, heat milk and butter together until very warm (120° to 125°F.). With an electric mixer, at low speed, beat milk mixture into dry ingredients until blended. Increase speed to medium and beat for 2 minutes. Beat in egg and 1 cup flour; beat 2 minutes longer, scraping down sides of bowl occasionally. With a spoon, stir in enough of remaining flour to make a stiff dough.

On a lightly floured surface, knead dough until well mixed, approximately 3 to 5 minutes. Place dough in a greased bowl, turning to coat entire surface. Cover with a clean towel; let rise in a warm, draft-free place 1 to 1½ hours, or until doubled in volume.

Punch dough down and place on a lightly floured surface. Cover and let rest 15 minutes.

With a lightly floured rolling pin, roll dough to scant ½-inch thickness.

With floured English muffin rings or empty 3½-inch tuna cans or a 3- to 4-inch biscuit cutter or glass, cut dough into circles. Reroll scraps until all dough is used.

Sprinkle cornmeal on a plate and dip both sides of each muffin to coat evenly with cornmeal. Place muffins on baking sheets; cover with a towel and let rise 45 minutes, or until doubled.

Lightly brush a large skillet with oil and heat over medium-high heat. When hot, add 5 to 6 muffins and reduce heat to medium. Cook 7 to 8 minutes on each side, or until muffins are golden. Remove to a rack to cool. Repeat with remaining muffins.

Let muffins cool completely and store in an airtight container. Split muffins with a fork and toast before serving.

English muffins freeze well.

Makes approximately 20 muffins

For Rye English Muffins: Substitute 2½ cups rye flour for 2½ cups all-purpose flour during the initial and electric-mixer phases of the recipe. Complete the recipe with 2 to 2½ cups all-purpose flour.

For Whole-Wheat English Muffins: Substitute 2½ cups whole-wheat flour for 2½ cups all-purpose flour during the initial and electric-mixer phases of the recipe. Complete the recipe with 2 to 2½ cups all-purpose flour.

For Cinnamon Raisin English Muffins: In any English muffin recipe, substitute ¼ cup firmly packed light-brown sugar for the 1 tablespoon sugar and add 1 teaspoon ground cinnamon to the yeast mixture. Stir in 1 cup raisins after electric-mixer phase of recipe.

· HAM AND CHEESE MUFFINS ·

1³/₄ cups all-purpose flour
¹/₃ cup rye flour
1 tablespoon firmly packed dark-brown
  sugar
2 teaspoons baking powder
¹/₄ teaspoon salt
¹/₂ cup (about 2¹/₂ ounces) finely
  chopped cooked ham
¹/₂ cup (about 2 ounces) shredded
  Swiss or Gruyère cheese

1 cup milk
¹/₄ cup vegetable oil
1 egg, lightly beaten
1 teaspoon prepared spicy brown
  mustard
¹/₄ teaspoon Worcestershire sauce
3 drops Tabasco

Preheat oven to 400°F. Grease ten 3 × 1¹/₄-inch (3¹/₂- to 4-ounce) muffin cups.

In a large bowl, stir together flours, brown sugar, baking powder, and salt; stir in ham and cheese to coat. In another bowl, stir together milk, oil, egg, mustard, Worcestershire, and Tabasco until blended. Make a well in center of dry ingredients; add milk mixture and stir just to combine.

Spoon batter into prepared muffin cups; bake 20 to 25 minutes, or until a cake tester inserted in center of one muffin comes out clean.

Remove muffin tin or tins to a wire rack. Cool 5 minutes before removing muffins from cups. Finish cooling on rack. Serve warm or cool completely and store in an airtight container in refrigerator. Let muffins reach room temperature or warm slightly before serving.

Makes 10 muffins

· IRISH SODA BREAD MUFFINS ·

2 cups all-purpose flour
3 tablespoons sugar
1 1/2 teaspoons baking powder
1/2 teaspoon baking soda
1/2 teaspoon salt
1/4 cup lightly salted butter or
    margarine

1 cup buttermilk
1 egg, lightly beaten
3/4 cup currants
1/2 teaspoon caraway seeds (optional)

Preheat oven to 375°F. Grease ten 3 × 1 1/4-inch (3 1/2- to 4-ounce) muffin cups.

In a large bowl, stir together flour, sugar, baking powder, baking soda, and salt. With pastry cutter or two knives used scissors fashion, cut in butter until mixture resembles coarse crumbs. In a small bowl, stir together buttermilk and egg until blended. Add buttermilk mixture to dry ingredients and stir to combine. Stir in currants and caraway seeds (if desired).

Spoon batter into prepared muffin cups. Bake 20 to 25 minutes, or until cake tester inserted in center of one muffin comes out clean.

Remove muffin tin or tins to wire rack. Cool 5 minutes before removing muffins from cups; finish cooling on rack. Serve warm or cool completely and store muffins in an airtight container at room temperature.

These muffins freeze well.

Makes 10 muffins

· MEXICAN MUFFINS ·

1 cup yellow cornmeal
1 cup all-purpose flour
2 teaspoons sugar
1¹/₂ teaspoons baking powder
¹/₂ teaspoon baking soda
¹/₈ teaspoon salt
¹/₂ cup (about 2 ounces) shredded
   Cheddar cheese

¹/₂ cup taco sauce
¹/₃ cup sour cream
1 egg, lightly beaten
3 tablespoons corn or vegetable oil
1 can (3 ounces) chopped green chilies,
   drained

Preheat oven to 400°F. Grease nine 3 × 1¹/₄-inch (3¹/₂- to 4-ounce) muffin cups.

In a large bowl, stir together cornmeal, flour, sugar, baking powder, baking soda, and salt; stir in cheese. In another bowl, stir together taco sauce, sour cream, egg, oil, and chilies until blended. Make a well in center of dry ingredients; add taco sauce mixture and stir just to combine./

Spoon batter into prepared muffin cups; bake 15 to 20 minutes, or until a cake tester inserted in center of one muffin comes out clean.

Remove muffin tin or tins to wire rack. Cool 5 minutes before removing muffins from cups; finish cooling on rack. Serve warm or cool completely and store in an airtight container in refrigerator. Let muffins reach room temperature or warm slightly before serving.

These muffins freeze well.

Makes 9 muffins

· PEPPERONI PIZZA MUFFINS ·

2 cups all-purpose flour
2 teaspoons sugar
2 teaspoons baking powder
1/4 teaspoon dried leaf oregano,
    crumbled
1/8 teaspoon salt
Dash ground red pepper (optional)
1/2 cup (about 2 ounces) shredded
    mozzarella cheese

2 tablespoons freshly grated Parmesan
    cheese
1/2 cup tomato sauce
1/3 cup milk
1 egg, lightly beaten
3 tablespoons lightly salted butter or
    margarine, melted and cooled
1/2 cup chopped pepperoni

Preheat oven to 400°F. Grease nine 3 × 1¼-inch (3½- to 4-ounce) muffin cups.

In a large bowl, stir together flour, sugar, baking powder, oregano, salt, and red pepper (if desired); stir in cheeses. In another bowl, stir together tomato sauce, milk, egg, and butter until blended. Make a well in center of dry ingredients; add tomato sauce mixture and stir just to combine. Stir in pepperoni.

Spoon batter into prepared muffin cups; bake 15 to 20 minutes, or until a cake tester inserted in center of one muffin comes out clean.

Remove muffin tin or tins to wire rack. Cool 5 minutes before removing muffins from cups; finish cooling on rack. Serve warm or cool completely and store in an airtight container in refrigerator. Let muffins reach room temperature or warm slightly before serving.

Makes 9 muffins

· POTATO DILL MUFFINS ·

2 cups all-purpose flour
1½ teaspoons baking powder
¼ teaspoon baking soda
½ teaspoon salt
¾ cup milk
½ cup sour cream
½ cup mashed, cooked potatoes

¼ cup lightly salted butter or
  margarine, melted and cooled
1 egg, lightly beaten
⅛ teaspoon Tabasco
2 tablespoons finely chopped scallions
2 tablespoons finely chopped fresh dill
  or ½ teaspoon dried dill

Preheat oven to 400°F. Grease twelve 3 × 1¼-inch (3½- to 4-ounce) muffin cups.

In a large bowl, stir together flour, baking powder, baking soda, and salt. In another bowl, stir together milk, sour cream, mashed potatoes, butter, egg, and Tabasco until blended. Make a well in center of dry ingredients; add milk mixture and stir just to combine. Stir in scallions and dill.

Batter will be sticky; spoon it into prepared muffin cups. Bake 15 to 20 minutes, or until a cake tester inserted in center of one muffin comes out clean.

Remove muffin tin or tins to wire rack. Cool 5 minutes before removing muffins from tins; finish cooling on rack. Serve warm or cool completely and store in an airtight container in refrigerator. Let muffins reach room temperature or warm slightly before serving.

These muffins freeze well.

Makes 12 muffins

· PROVOLONE RYE MUFFINS ·

1 cup all-purpose flour
1 cup rye flour
1 1/2 teaspoons baking powder
1/2 teaspoon baking soda
1/4 teaspoon salt
1 1/3 cups (about 5 1/2 ounces) shredded
    provolone cheese
1 cup buttermilk

1/4 cup vegetable oil
1 egg, lightly beaten
2 tablespoons molasses
1/2 teaspoon Dijon-style mustard
1/2 teaspoon caraway seeds (optional)
1/2 teaspoon Worcestershire sauce
1/8 teaspoon ground black pepper

Preheat oven to 400°F. Grease twelve 3 × 1 1/4-inch (3 1/2- to 4-ounce) muffin cups.

In a large bowl, stir together flours, baking powder, baking soda, and salt; stir in cheese to coat. In another bowl, stir together buttermilk, oil, egg, molasses, mustard, caraway seeds (if desired), Worcestershire, and pepper until blended. Make a well in center of dry ingredients; add buttermilk mixture and stir just to combine.

Spoon batter into prepared muffin cups; bake 15 to 20 minutes, or until a cake tester inserted in center of one muffin comes out clean.

Remove muffin tin or tins to wire rack. Cool 5 minutes before removing muffins from cups; finish cooling on rack. Serve warm or cool completely and store in an airtight container in refrigerator. Let muffins reach room temperature or warm slightly before serving.

Makes 12 muffins

· SAUSAGE APPLE MUFFINS ·

Great with cocktails or served with meals.

2 cups all-purpose flour
1 tablespoon firmly packed dark-brown
  sugar
2¹/₂ teaspoons baking powder
¹/₄ teaspoon salt
¹/₈ teaspoon ground black pepper
Dash ground nutmeg
1 cup (about 4 ounces) shredded Swiss
  cheese

¹/₂ cup dry white wine
¹/₃ cup vegetable oil
¹/₄ cup water
1 egg, lightly beaten
¹/₂ teaspoon prepared spicy brown
  mustard
¹/₂ pound bulk pork sausage, cooked,
  drained, cooled, and crumbled
1 cup diced apple

Preheat oven to 375°F. Grease twelve 3 × 1¹/₄-inch (3¹/₂- to 4-ounce) muffin cups.

In a large bowl, stir together flour, brown sugar, baking powder, salt, pepper, and nutmeg. Stir in cheese to coat. In another bowl, stir together wine, oil, water, egg, and mustard. Make a well in center of dry ingredients; add wine mixture and stir just to combine. Stir in sausage and apple.

Spoon batter into prepared muffin cups; bake 15 to 20 minutes, or until a cake tester inserted in center of one muffin comes out clean.

Remove to wire rack. Cool 5 minutes before removing muffins from cups; finish cooling on rack. Serve warm or cool completely and store in an airtight container in refrigerator. Let muffins reach room temperature or warm slightly before serving.

Makes 12 muffins

· ZUCCHINI CARROT ONION MUFFINS ·

This vegetable-trio muffin makes an interesting accompaniment to dinner.

1/4 cup lightly salted butter or
margarine
1/2 cup shredded zucchini
1/2 cup shredded carrot
1/4 cup finely chopped onion
1/2 teaspoon dried thyme

2 1/2 cups all-purpose flour
2 teaspoons sugar
1 1/2 teaspoons baking soda
3/4 teaspoon salt
1 1/2 cups buttermilk
1 egg, lightly beaten

Preheat oven to 400°F. Grease twelve 3 × 1 1/4-inch (3 1/2- to 4-ounce) muffin cups.

In a small saucepan, melt butter; add zucchini, carrot, onion, and thyme and cook 5 to 7 minutes, or until vegetables are softened.

In a large bowl, stir together flour, sugar, baking soda, and salt. In another bowl, stir together buttermilk, egg, and vegetable mixture. Make a well in center of dry ingredients; add buttermilk mixture and stir just to combine.

Spoon batter into prepared muffin cups; bake 25 to 30 minutes, or until a cake tester inserted in center of one muffin comes out clean.

Remove muffin tin or tins to wire rack. Cool 5 minutes before removing muffins from cups; finish cooling on rack. Serve warm or cool completely and store in an airtight container in refrigerator. Let muffins reach room temperature or warm slightly before serving.

These muffins freeze well.

Makes 12 muffins

Spreads

· APRICOT PECAN SPREAD ·

³/₄ cup (about 20) dried apricot halves
1 cup water
¹/₂ cup chopped pecans
1 package (7¹/₂ ounces) farmer cheese

3 tablespoons firmly packed
   dark-brown sugar
¹/₄ teaspoon vanilla

In a small saucepan, combine apricots and water. Bring to a boil; boil 1 minute. Remove from heat; let stand 10 minutes.

Drain apricots; place in container of food processor fitted with steel blade. Process 30 seconds, or until puréed. Add pecans; process 30 seconds, or until nuts are ground. Add farmer cheese, brown sugar, and vanilla. Process 30 seconds, or until smooth, stopping to scrape down sides of container with rubber scraper, if necessary.

Remove spread to a small bowl. Serve immediately or cover and refrigerate. To serve, let stand 15 minutes at room temperature to soften.

Makes approximately 1¹/₂ cups

• BEER CHEESE SPREAD •

Great with crudités, too!

2 cups (about 8 ounces) shredded Swiss
    cheese
4 ounces cream cheese, softened
1 teaspoon Dijon-style mustard

1 teaspoon Worcestershire sauce
1/2 teaspoon Tabasco
1/4 cup beer

In a medium bowl, beat Swiss cheese and cream cheese with an electric mixer until combined; beat in mustard, Worcestershire, and Tabasco. Gradually beat in beer, a little at a time, beating well after each addition. Cover and chill spread at least 24 hours to develop flavor. To serve, let stand 15 minutes at room temperature to soften.

Makes approximately 1 1/3 cups

· BLUE-CHEESE BRIE SPREAD ·

²/₃ cup (about 2¹/₂ ounces) trimmed Brie, softened
1 package (3 ounces) cream cheese, softened

2 ounces blue cheese, crumbled
2 tablespoons unsalted butter, softened
¹/₄ cup chopped walnuts

Place Brie, cream cheese, blue cheese, and butter in container of food processor fitted with steel blade; process 30 seconds, or until smooth, stopping to scrape down sides of container with rubber scraper, if necessary. Add walnuts; process 30 seconds, or until combined.

Remove spread to a small bowl. Serve immediately or cover and refrigerate. To serve, let stand 15 minutes at room temperature to soften.

Makes approximately 1¹/₃ cups

• BROWN-SUGAR CINNAMON BUTTER •

*¹/₄ cup lightly salted butter or
   margarine, softened
2 teaspoons firmly packed light-brown*

*sugar
¹/₈ teaspoon ground cinnamon*

In a small bowl, mix together butter, brown sugar, and cinnamon until thoroughly combined.

Serve spread immediately or cover and refrigerate. To serve, let stand 15 minutes at room temperature to soften.

Makes approximately ¹/₄ cup

• CREAM CHEESE SPREAD •

*2 packages (3 ounces each) cream
   cheese, softened
1 tablespoon lightly salted butter or
   margarine, softened*

*¹/₃ cup confectioners sugar
¹/₄ teaspoon vanilla
Dash ground mace*

In a medium bowl, stir together all ingredients until smooth.

Serve spread immediately or cover and refrigerate. To serve, let stand 15 minutes at room temperature to soften.

Makes approximately 1 cup

· ESPRESSO SPREAD ·

4 ounces cream cheese, softened
1 square (1 ounce) semisweet chocolate,
  grated

1 tablespoon sugar
1/2 teaspoon vanilla
1/2 teaspoon instant espresso powder

Place cheese, chocolate, sugar, vanilla, and espresso in container of food processor fitted with steel blade; process 30 seconds, or until smooth, stopping to scrape down sides of container with rubber scraper, if necessary.

Remove spread to a small bowl. Serve immediately or cover and refrigerate. To serve, let stand 10 minutes at room temperature to soften.

Makes approximately 1 1/2 cups

· HAWAIIAN SPREAD ·

¹/₂ cup salted, roasted macadamia nuts
¹/₂ cup chopped, peeled mango or
  papaya
4 ounces cream cheese, softened

3 tablespoons pineapple preserves
2 tablespoons lightly salted butter or
  margarine, softened
¹/₄ teaspoon vanilla

Place nuts in container of food processor fitted with steel blade; process 30 seconds, or until ground. Add mango; process 30 seconds, or until puréed. Add cream cheese, preserves, butter, and vanilla; process 30 seconds, or until smooth, stopping to scrape down sides of container with rubber scraper, if necessary.

Remove spread to a small bowl. Cover and refrigerate 1 hour, or until chilled and slightly firm.

Makes approximately 1¹/₃ cups

• HAZELNUT CREAM-CHEESE SPREAD •

1 package (3 ounces) cream cheese,
  softened
2 teaspoons hazelnut-flavored liqueur

1 1/2 teaspoons sugar
2 tablespoons finely chopped hazelnuts

In a small bowl, mix together cream cheese, liqueur, and sugar until thoroughly combined; stir in hazelnuts.

Serve spread immediately or cover and refrigerate. To serve, let stand 15 minutes at room temperature to soften.

Makes approximately 1/3 cup

• LEMON BOURBON BUTTER •

1/2 cup lightly salted butter or
  margarine, softened
2 tablespoons confectioners sugar

2 teaspoons bourbon
1/4 teaspoon grated lemon peel
1 teaspoon freshly squeezed lemon juice

In a small bowl, stir together butter, sugar, bourbon, lemon peel, and lemon juice until smooth.

Serve spread immediately or cover and refrigerate. To serve, let stand 20 minutes at room temperature to soften.

Makes approximately 1/2 cup

· LEMON CURD (ENGLISH LEMON SPREAD) ·

In addition to being perfect with muffins, lemon curd is also delicious on toast, English muffins, and poundcake.

3/4 cup plus 2 tablespoons sugar
3/4 cup freshly squeezed lemon juice
1/3 cup unsalted (sweet) butter, cut into

1/2-inch pieces
1 tablespoon grated lemon peel
4 eggs

In a medium saucepan over medium heat, cook sugar, lemon juice, butter, and lemon peel until sugar dissolves and butter melts, stirring occasionally. In a medium bowl, beat eggs until light and fluffy. Very gradually add heated mixture to eggs, beating constantly. Return mixture to saucepan and heat, stirring constantly, until mixture thickens.

Pour mixture into a heatproof glass container. Cool, then cover and refrigerate until slightly thicker.

Makes approximately 2 cups

· LEMON GLAZE ·

1 cup confectioners sugar

1 tablespoon freshly squeezed lemon juice

In a small bowl, stir juice into sugar until smooth. Drizzle approximately 1 teaspoon over each muffin.

Makes approximately 1/4 cup

· NUT BUTTER ·

6 ounces unsalted roasted cashews,
  roasted peanuts without skins, or
  blanched slivered almonds

2 teaspoons peanut or vegetable oil
$1/4$ teaspoon sugar
$1/8$ to $1/4$ teaspoon salt

Place nuts, oil, sugar, and salt in container of food processor fitted with steel blade; process $2^{1}/_{2}$ to 3 minutes, or until smooth, stopping to scrape down sides of container with rubber scraper, if necessary.

Remove butter to small bowl. Serve immediately or cover and refrigerate. Let stand at room temperature to soften, if necessary.

Makes approximately $2/3$ to $3/4$ cup

Note: For variation, almonds can be toasted. To toast, place almonds in single layer on baking sheet or jelly-roll pan. Bake at 350°F for 6 to 7 minutes, or until lightly browned, stirring once or twice.

One-quarter teaspoon molasses may be substituted for the sugar in cashew or peanut butter.

• NUTTED CHEESE SPREAD •

1 package (8 ounces) cream cheese,
* softened*
2 tablespoons chopped walnuts

1 tablespoon confectioners sugar
¹/₄ teaspoon vanilla

Place cheese, walnuts, sugar, and vanilla in container of food processor fitted with steel blade; process 30 seconds, or until smooth, stopping to scrape down sides of container with rubber scraper, if necessary.

Remove spread to a small bowl. Serve immediately or cover and refrigerate. To serve, let stand 15 minutes at room temperature to soften.

Makes approximately 1 cup

• ORANGE HONEY BUTTER •

¹/₂ cup lightly salted butter or
* margarine, softened*
1¹/₂ teaspoons honey
1¹/₂ tablespoons frozen concentrated

orange juice, thawed, undiluted
¹/₈ teaspoon grated orange peel
* (optional)*

In a small bowl, beat butter until light and smooth. Add honey and continue to beat until well combined. Gradually beat in orange juice concentrate and orange peel (if desired).

Cover and chill spread several hours to blend flavors.

Makes approximately ¹/₂ cup

• ORANGE PECAN CREAM-CHEESE SPREAD •

1 package (3 ounces) cream cheese,
  softened
1½ teaspoons sugar

1 teaspoon orange-flavored liqueur
2 tablespoons finely chopped pecans

In a small bowl, stir together cream cheese, sugar, and liqueur; stir in pecans.

Serve spread immediately or cover and refrigerate. To serve, let stand 15 minutes at room temperature to soften.

Makes approximately ⅓ cup

• RAISIN NUT CREAM-CHEESE SPREAD •

1 package (8 ounces) cream cheese,
  softened
⅓ cup chopped walnuts or pecans

⅓ cup raisins
1 teaspoon honey
⅛ teaspoon ground cinnamon

Place cheese, nuts, raisins, honey, and cinnamon in container of food processor fitted with steel blade; process 30 seconds, or until smooth, stopping to scrape down sides of container with rubber scraper, if necessary.

Remove spread to a small bowl. Serve immediately or cover and refrigerate. To serve, let stand 15 minutes at room temperature to soften.

Makes approximately 1⅓ cups

• PEACH SPREAD •

1 package (7¹/₂ ounces) farmer cheese
¹/₂ cup chopped, peeled fresh peaches
   or thawed, frozen, drained peaches
1 tablespoon toasted slivered almonds
   (see note below)

2 to 3 teaspoons honey
¹/₄ teaspoon vanilla
Dash ground cinnamon
Dash ground ginger

Place cheese, peaches, almonds, honey, vanilla, cinnamon, and ginger in container of food processor fitted with steel blade; process 30 seconds, or until smooth, stopping to scrape down sides of container with rubber scraper, if necessary.

Remove spread to a small bowl. Cool to room temperature and serve immediately or cover and refrigerate.

Makes approximately 1¹/₄ cups

Note: To toast almonds, place in small skillet over medium-high heat. Cook, stirring, 3 minutes, or until lightly browned.

· RAISIN WALNUT YOGURT-CHEESE SPREAD ·

1 container (32 ounces) plain yogurt
1/4 cup finely chopped walnuts
1/4 cup chopped raisins

1 tablespoon sugar
1/4 teaspoon vanilla
Dash ground cinnamon

Line a colander or strainer with cheesecloth or a clean dish towel. Place colander in sink or over a bowl. Spoon yogurt into center of colander and gather up edges of towel. Drain yogurt overnight or at least 6 hours at room temperature; the longer the yogurt drains, the firmer the finished cheese will be.

In a medium bowl, stir together drained yogurt, walnuts, raisins, sugar, vanilla, and cinnamon until blended. Serve immediately or cover and refrigerate.

Makes approximately 1 1/2 cups

· TAHINI PEANUT-BUTTER SPREAD ·

¹/₄ cup tahini (sesame seed paste,
available in health food stores,
Middle Eastern markets, and
foreign food sections of large
supermarkets)

¹/₄ cup peanut butter
1 tablespoon molasses
1 teaspoon honey

In a small bowl, stir together tahini, peanut butter, molasses, and honey until smooth.

Serve spread immediately or cover and refrigerate. To serve, let stand 10 minutes at room temperature to soften.

Makes approximately ¹/₂ cup

Create Your
Own Muffins

As you can see, this versatile baked product lends itself to many variations. The preceding recipes can be modified slightly. For example, you can substitute chopped dried apricots or dates, and so on, for raisins or change the type of nuts to give the muffins your personal touch.

The following basic muffin recipe will give you a starting point from which to develop your own ideas. By substituting various flours for part of the all-purpose flour, the texture of the batter and baked muffin will change along with the flavor. Cornmeal will produce a coarser-grained product with a crumbly texture, while whole-wheat flour yields a coarser, denser muffin with a slightly nutty flavor. Bran, oatmeal, and wheat germ give a chewy texture.

Don't be afraid to experiment—by trial and error you'll develop your own unique combinations. Let your tastebuds be your guide to flavor combinations. For sweet muffins, dried fruits, nuts, and spices can be juggled to create interesting variations. For savory muffins, cheeses, mustard, herbs, and spices plus additions of cooked vegetables, cooked ham, sausage or bacon—even nuts—can be added in various combinations for tasty results.

With a little imagination and the following guidelines, you're ready to begin.

· BASIC MUFFINS ·

2 cups all-purpose flour
1/4 to 1/2 cup sugar (see note below)
2 1/2 teaspoons baking powder
1/2 teaspoon salt
1 cup milk

1/4 to 1/2 cup lightly salted butter or
   margarine, melted and cooled, or
   vegetable oil (see note below)
1 egg, lightly beaten

Preheat oven to 400°F. Grease twelve 3 × 1 1/4-inch (3 1/2- to 4-ounce) muffin cups.

In a large bowl, stir together flour, sugar, baking powder, and salt. In another bowl, stir together milk, butter, and egg. Make a well in center of dry ingredients; add milk mixture and stir just to combine.

Spoon batter into prepared muffin cups; bake 15 to 20 minutes, or until a cake tester inserted in center of one muffin comes out clean.

Remove muffin tin or tins to wire rack. Cool 5 minutes before removing muffins from cups; finish cooling on rack. Serve warm or cool completely and store in an airtight container at room temperature.

Basic muffins freeze well.

Makes 12 muffins

Notes: For sweeter muffins, use 1/3 cup or 1/2 cup sugar; for savory muffins, decrease sugar to 2 tablespoons or less.

For richer muffins, use 1/3 cup or 1/2 cup butter, margarine, or oil.

· SUBSTITUTIONS ·

FLOUR:

For up to 1 cup all-purpose flour, an equal amount of whole-wheat flour, cornmeal, or rye flour.

For up to 1/2 cup all-purpose flour, an equal amount of unprocessed bran, wheat germ, or rolled oats.

SWEETENERS:

For granulated sugar, equal amounts of firmly packed light-brown or dark-brown sugar.

For part of the sugar, honey or molasses (in large amounts, the liquid component of the recipe will have to be reduced accordingly).

• ADDITIONS TO SWEET MUFFINS •

FRUIT:

¹/₃ cup to 1 cup currants, raisins, or chopped dried fruit such as dates, prunes, apricots, pineapple, pears, and apples

¹/₄ teaspoon grated orange or lemon peel

NUTS:

¹/₃ cup to ²/₃ cup peanuts, cashews, pine nuts, or chopped nuts such as almonds, pecans, walnuts, macadamia nuts, Brazil nuts, and mixed nuts. (Baking nuts at 350°F for 5 to 7 minutes or until golden will add a toasted flavor.)

EXTRACTS AND LIQUEURS:

1 teaspoon vanilla

¹/₄ teaspoon almond, rum, brandy, or maple extract

1 to 2 tablespoons brandy, rum, bourbon, or your favorite liqueur, adjusting liquid accordingly

SPICES:

¹/₄ to ¹/₂ teaspoon ground cinnamon

¹/₈ teaspoon ground allspice, cloves, ginger, mace, or nutmeg

MISCELLANEOUS:

¹/₂ cup to 1 cup chocolate chips, peanut butter chips, or butterscotch chips, or a combination

2 tablespoons toasted sesame seeds

1/2 to 1 cup (about 2 to 4 ounces) shredded hard cheese, such as Cheddar, Swiss, or provolone

1 teaspoon to 1 tablespoon Dijon-style mustard or prepared spicy brown mustard

1/4 teaspoon dry mustard

1/4 to 1/2 teaspoon dried thyme, oregano, or basil

1/4 to 1/2 teaspoon caraway seeds or dried rosemary, dill, or sage

Dash to 1/8 teaspoon ground black pepper

Dash ground red pepper

2 to 3 drops Tabasco

1 small clove garlic, minced

1/2 to 1 teaspoon Worcestershire sauce

1/4 to 1/2 cup chopped onion, red or green pepper, or celery, sautéed in 1 tablespoon butter, margarine, or oil

1/4 to 1/2 cup shredded zucchini, yellow summer squash or carrots, squeezed dry

1/4 to 1 cup fresh corn, or thawed, drained, frozen whole-kernel corn

2 tablespoons toasted sesame seeds

1/3 to 2/3 cup chopped nuts

Index